Reclaiming My Hope

Surviving Birmingham's Sixteenth Street Baptist Church
Bombing in 1963, a Day That Shamed the Nation

Dr. Ethel Madison Van Buren

ISBN 979-8-88616-095-6 (paperback)
ISBN 979-8-88616-096-3 (digital)

Christian Faith Publishing
832 Park Avenue
Meadville, PA 16335
www.christianfaithpublishing.com

Printed in the United States of America

Praises for *Reclaiming My Hope*

"Dr. Ethel Van Buren gives a compelling first-hand account for what it means to stare down racist and hate-filled demons who bombed the beloved Sixteenth Street Baptist Church on that dreadful Sunday morning, September 15, 1963. Personally, knowing each of the girls who were killed drove the sword of pain and despair even deeper into the indelible memory of the writer, and those of us who loved them, making their killing all the more horrific!

This book should remind us of our shameful past as Americans, and encourage us to trust higher in our expectation of the greater goods. As the writer suggests, "Racism still plagues us. Even today, our nation appears raw and racially divided more than it has been since the Civil Rights Movement." I agree with Dr. Van Buren, we do need to ask the question, "Is our nation on the verge of allowing the Jim Crow idolatry to resurface in our society?" I suspect the reality of our responses might prove disheartening and even frightening.

Good job, Dr. Van Buren, you have provoked us to think!"

Dr. E. Victoria Williams, *Lifelong Friend*
Former Member and Board of Trustees,
Sixteenth Street Baptist Church
CEO, Blanton-Cody Enterprises, LLC

"The author poignantly tells her story of survival by conveying her factual, first-hand, emotional perspective of the Sixteenth Street Baptist Church bombing in Birmingham, Alabama in the early 1960s. This story is told through the eyes of the author, who was a young teenager at the time. Despite surviving the horrific tragedy, she also cites the difficulties that Black Americans experienced living through the scourge of racism in the segregated south, and the long reaching effect that it had on the human soul and spirit. This memoir is compelling …you will not be able to put it down until every single page has been read."

Kathy Yates, *Friend*
Atlanta, Georgia

"Dr. Ethel Van Buren revealed a phenomenal story of survival, perseverance, faith, and hope during a time in American history when cultural obstacles were in place to deter a move forward. I'm honored to be your friend. Dr. Van Buren is a rare and extraordinary woman who wrote a moving and genuine story about herself. May God continue to bless and guide you on your journey of reclaiming your hope. Congratulation! Wishing you much success with the book."

Larry B. Taylor, *Friend*
Former Assistant Director, Gust Experience & Operations
Atlanta Hawks Basketball Club & State Farm Arena

"Dr. Ethel Van Buren, my dear friend, so proud of your accomplishment. I am happy that you completed your manuscript for publication. Your confidence, persistence, and faith in God ensured your success. I am looking forward to reading and enjoying the finished product."

Dr. Jacquelyn Woods-Thompson, *Friend*
Retired Atlanta Public Schools Administrator

"Kudos Ethel for giving an incredible account of what you experienced on that horrendous day when Birmingham's Sixteenth Street Baptist Church was bombed."

Carolyn Drakeford, *Friend*
Retired Atlanta Public Schools Educator

"An engaging read that provides insights into the influences of Dr. Van Buren's life … Revealing and enduring."

Dr. Gloria Neltine Peebles- Patterson, *Friend*
Retired Atlanta Public Schools Administrator

"Auntie Ethel, I know it took courage to tell your account about a difficult destiny in your life. I know that my mom, your sister, Ann, is smiling down on you with great joy and happiness on your accomplishment. I'm so proud that you are courageously sharing your story.

Wishing you much success with this book. Congratulation! Much Love."

Juan Johnson, *Beloved Nephew*
Sr. Traction Power Engineer
Metro, Washington, DC

To my late parents, Edmond and Annie Woods
Madison, I am filled with hope from your guidance
to be open to the will of God in all ways.

To my late son, Jermayne Montiel Van Buren, I am filled with
peace now knowing that your soul is being nourished by God.

To my late sister, Annie "Ann" Madison Johnson, I
can smile now with joy and be filled with gladness
because you were all that I needed you to be.

To my brother, Edmond Madison Jr., I pray that
you continue to express God's strength, wisdom,
power, and love in your life every day.

In memory of my four friends killed in the church bombing: Addie Mae Collins, Carol Robertson, Cynthia Wesley, and Denise McNair. I believe now that your deaths were not in vain.

Contents

Preface

As I look back, it is hard to believe that fifty-plus years have gone by since I sat on the pew at Sixteenth Street Baptist Church just minutes before the bomb exploded on September 15, 1963, at 10:22 a.m. I was fifteen years old, just starting my third year in high school, and excited about some of the positive changes that were unfolding in the city of Birmingham, Alabama, as a result of the Birmingham campaign for civil rights during April and May in 1963.

I have always had the compelling urge to give my eyewitness account of that day. Even though fifty-plus years have passed, the image of that day is still fresh in my mind as if it happened yesterday. The pain, shock, and disbelief still linger. For a long time after that day, I carried the burden of hurt and fear in my heart. But my faith and God's favor have kept me going since that day. With faith, I have been able to release the burden and reconstruct my idea of hope.

I casually shared the event of that day with friends and colleagues over the years, and some of them have said to me, "You have a story to tell." But that was a time and event that I was trying to forget but couldn't. I consider it a blessing from God to be able to share my eyewitness account and feelings about that horrible day and time in our nation's history and the impact that it had on my life. Journalists and reporters have given their views about the bombing event. Authors and historians have written books and film producers have presented documentaries that tried to depict what happened that day. Only those of us who were there that day and survived can really tell the story. My perception of that day is a forever memory that will never go away no matter how many years have passed. Everything that I have experienced and done in life, I believe, is because of divine order. However, it is difficult for me to believe that the event that took place on Sunday, September 15, 1963, at 10:22 a.m., happened because of divine order. Yet it happened. I have been taught to believe that God is always in control no matter what happens. There are no coincidences. Nothing happens by chance. God is beyond my comprehension, which means I will never understand or know why that horrible event came into my life on that given day. Perhaps God wanted to use an ordinary person like me to tell the story through my eyes.

I was empowered and enthusiastic about taking part in the Children's Crusade march under the leadership of Dr. Martin Luther King Jr. on May 2, 1963, when I narrowly escaped the water from the fire hoses that the Birmingham Fire Department used to stop the protesters from walking through Kelly Ingram Park to get to the downtown area. Kelly Ingram Park is a public park located directly across the street from Sixteenth Street Baptist Church that Black Americans were not allowed to visit or walk through during the Jim Crow era. I could not believe what my eyes were seeing as I watched the inhumane actions of the Birmingham Police Officers using vicious German shepherd dogs to attack some of the nonviolent children who were on the front line of the protest. That painful image will be etched in my mind forever.

Birmingham, Alabama, was a place where Black Americans endured unequal treatment on all levels of human rights—the rights to life and liberty, freedom from discrimination and torture, fairness, equality, respect, independence, and many more. In the early 1960s, Birmingham was one of the most racially divided cities in the United States. Black Americans faced unlawful and economic disparities on every level and received violent retribution when attempting to bring attention to the inequality. Segregation of public and commercial facilities was rigidly enforced throughout the city. Black Americans were not allowed to go into the main district of downtown Birmingham except on certain days. White-owned retail stores like Woolworth's, Pizitz, Loveman's, and Sears, Roebuck and Company did allow Black Americans to shop in restricted areas of their stores. The basement sections of Pizitz, Woolworth, and Loveman's were designated for Black Americans to shop, where the lower quality goods were sold.

However, there was a small section of downtown Birmingham allocated on Fourth Avenue North between Seventeenth and Eighteenth Streets for Black-owned businesses.

These disparities led black Americans in Birmingham to organize to bring about change. Civil rights leaders met at Black churches to discuss issues related to the injustices and racial turmoil to come up with strategies to reconcile the injustice. Those churches became specific targets for attack. Sixteenth Street Baptist Church was the headquarters and rendezvous point for the Birmingham Campaign. The Birmingham Campaign was a strategic movement organized by the Southern Christian Leadership Conference (SCLC) that laid out the plans to manage and direct the nonviolent protest against the injustices imposed on Black Americans in the city. The church leaders received a warning that the church would be bombed if they continued to use the church as a rallying point for the protestors. In spite of the warnings, the church leaders continued to let the protestors meet and strategize.

The memory of that time in history is still painful to talk and think about. Even though over fifty-plus years have passed and we have come a long way as a society, the scars of racism are still embedded in my mind. I have been rejected, hated, oppressed, and almost killed in the church bombing. But thank God my life was spared to see another day. I can truly say that I am blessed to be able to see the changes in the city of Birmingham and our nation brought about through the Civil Rights Movement. Although a lot has changed in Birmingham, Alabama, and the nation regarding civil rights, racism continues to plague us. Even today, our nation appears raw and racially divided more than it has been since the Civil Rights Movement. Makes me ask the question, "Is our nation on the verge of allowing the Jim Crow idolatry to resurface in our society?"

I wrote this book through my voice about my life experiences during the Jim Crow era when the concept of "separate but equal" permeated the entire Southland of our nation, and the impact it made on my heart, mind, and soul. The way Black Americans were treated in the Southland during that time is unspeakable, yet it is the reality of our history. In spite of our history, we all have a common thread: hope, liberty, justice, and freedom. An American sociologist, historian, civil rights activist, and author W. E. B. Du Bois said it this way: "The cost of liberty is less than the price of repression." The "separate but equal" policy was an act of using force to control the will and desires of Black Americans. The laws were created to make us believe that we were unable to act upon our desires and aspirations. Our self-dignity, self-respect, and self-esteem were enslaved by those laws. The Civil Rights Movement helped us acknowledge our liberty as the God-given right that it is.

I hope my account of the unforgettable day that shamed the nation and the ugly truth about life during the Jim Crow era will inspire and fill your heart with compassion and empathy. As a Christian, I have the Spirit as my guiding source to help me plant positive seeds in the fertile soil of my mind. Because of the Spirit, I have been able to release some of the painful memories of the past.

It may sound crazy to talk about Jim Crow today. But Jim Crow is not dead. Race, justice, and equality are issues in our society today that we are uncomfortable having a real honest, open, and frank dialogue about. Most of us want to pretend that maybe that era did not really happen and we are now color blind. But in reality, that era continues to shape our lives today. If we don't change our hearts and minds soon, our nation will become more fractured than it was in the past.

In this memoir, I give my description of how the ugly truths about segregation and discrimination during the early '50s and late '60s until the present day impacted my life. I describe how the unforgettable day that shamed the nation unfolded before my very eyes, my accounts of unforgettable events leading up to that day, and the aftermath. The remainder of the book gives my reflections about hope for justice, peace, healing, and reconciliation. My words on the pages within are honest and straightforward. I utilized the wisdom and the knowledge that I learned during my journey through life to convey my true feelings. Being able to tell my story has helped me to move peacefully beyond the painful memories of the darkness of the past into the light of change. I have learned how to fuel my thoughts with positive possibilities because divine order prevails in my mind and my life. And I do believe that God is the source of all prosperity, and I give thanks in advance knowing that my highest good is unfolding now. I have moved beyond the mind-set of powerlessness to seeing life through forgiving eyes. Yet the memories of the ugly events of the past, I will never forget. Because on an underlying level, racism still plagues our society.

Part 1

The Ugly Truth

Chapter 1

An honest witness tells the truth.

—Proverbs 12:17

Birmingham, Alabama. Sunday morning, September 15, 1963, at 10:22 a.m. is a day and time in history that cannot be forgotten by me, the citizens of Birmingham, along with millions of Americans all over the world. The heartbreak and pain of that day and time when evil-hearted individuals interrupted the worship service in God's house left a stain on the city of Birmingham, the state of Alabama, our nation, and the world. That was the day when I had to start searching for ways to reclaim my hope. The hope for justice, peace, healing, and reconciliation that I hold in my heart for me and the entire world. I needed to believe that hope is the seed that has the potential to bear good fruit. I needed to believe that hope is patience working its course. I needed the kind of hope that functions like a reservoir of emotional strength. I was anticipating a favorable outcome that would wipe out the ugly truth about racism. I really needed to feel hope in my heart to forgive instead of retaliating.

Before that unforgettable day that shamed the nation, life consisted of events and circumstances that made living in Birmingham, Alabama, a little frightening and sometimes unsafe for Black Americans in the city. The Jim Crow way of life sometimes made me doubt and not feel good about myself. I thank God for my loving parents, who helped me believe that the world was waiting for me to become all that I could become. Even though the Jim Crow way of life was designed to create fear and control our daily lives with barriers and restrictions. My spiritual upbringing also helped me confront the things and situations that made me fearful by believing that the Spirit of God is with me all the time protecting me from harm and danger.

In 1963, the Black communities in the city of Birmingham decided to take charge of fear and unleash the power of the spirit within and no longer be bound by the Jim Crow laws. During April and May, Sixteenth Street Baptist Church was the designated gathering place for the Civil Rights demonstrators, who decided that institutionalized racism which was widespread throughout the city needed to end. The size and location of the church made it an ideal location for the demonstrators to gather and march to the downtown Birmingham commercial district, municipal buildings, and parks. Sixteenth Street Baptist Church was considered a prestigious place of worship for Black Americans. I was baptized in the church on Easter Sunday in 1954. I was six years old when I gave my heart and soul to Jesus Christ as my Lord and Savior. At that time, I did not realize the complexity of my actions. To me, being baptized meant I would be able to take part in the Holy Communion service with the adults of the church on every first Sunday of the month. Participating in the communion service was very special to me once I fully understood the meaning and what it represented.

Sixteenth Street Baptist Church was organized as the first Colored Baptist Church of Birmingham, Alabama, in 1873. The present building was designed by the prominent Black architect Wallace Rayfield and constructed by the Windham Brothers and completed in 1911. As one of the primary institutions in the Black community, Sixteenth Street Baptist had hosted prominent visitors throughout its history. Such dignitaries included W. E. B. DuBois, Mary McLeod Bethune, Paul Robeson, Jackie Robinson, Ralph Bunche, and Dr. Martin Luther Jr. All spoke at the church during the first part of the twentieth century. The sanctuary also served as one of the largest auditoriums available to the Black citizens of Birmingham. Concerts by notable artists such as W. C. Handy frequently used the church for evening events. I felt proud and honored to be a member.

Growing up with Southern Christian values, I felt that going to church was an exciting and spiritual event that helped to develop a sense of community and family. Preparation for Sunday began on Saturday. Saturday was the day we studied our Sunday school lesson, which meant no listening to the radio or watching TV after five o'clock in the evening because we had to be in bed by eight o'clock. My family and I lived in a modest two-bedroom house with a living room, kitchen, and one bath with a screened front porch. My older sister Ann and I shared the same room and bed until she went off to college in 1964. Even though my sister and I were close siblings who very rarely disagreed with each other, we drew an invisible line down the middle of the double-sized bed to claim our individual sides. We always managed to respect each other's space.

Ann was very smart. She was a straight A student from first grade through high school. I admired her smarts, but at the same time, I felt a little intimidated. She won spelling bee contests while in elementary school and debates and science fair contests in high school. In addition to her being one of the two valedictorians, she was voted the most likely to succeed, the smartest and prettiest girl in her senior class at A. H. Parker High School, which was one of four high schools in Birmingham designated for Black students during that time.

In spite of the separate and unequal conditions in the public schools in Birmingham, the feeling of inferiority generated by White Americans was at a very low level in our school. We took pride in learning. Our teachers and parents taught us to believe in ourselves. In my household, there was no such thing as bringing home any grade less than a B. It was very hard for me to follow in my sister's footsteps. I was an honor student but not with straight As. My primary interest was in classical ballet, tap dance, and modern dance. However, I did not have the complete support of my parents to help me pursue that dream. They allowed me to take dance lessons on Saturdays from the time I was in the seventh grade through my high school years. But my dad always insisted that getting a good education was the best way to be successful in life.

In spite of the conditions for Black Americans in the South during that time, I had high hopes and dreams of becoming a famous ballerina. I wanted the world to know me. Even though all the ballerinas I saw on television did not look like me, I dreamed that I would be the first "Colored" girl to share the stage with the blonde-and-blue-eyed girls. I never understood why the color of a person's skin and the texture and length of your hair placed so many restrictions on what you could accomplish in life. We are all God's children, and if you have the talent and skills to perform, the color of your skin should not be a barrier. But I held on to my dream that anything is possible with faith and hope. Because having hope helps to prepare the way for good things to happen.

My parents met and married after my dad had served his time with the US Army during World War II. He did not tell me and my sister any memorable war stories. He told us that the experience of living in foxholes and jumping out of fighter planes in unknown territory was a time in his life that he would not like to relive under any circumstances. I also remember him mentioning that it was a time in history that should never be repeated. However, at the end of the war, the attitudes of some White Americans had changed toward Blacks after they had fought side by side with each other for the same cause. But, on the other hand, Black soldiers did not receive the same recognition for their courage, bravery, and service like the White soldiers.

My father was gentle, soft-spoken, and very intelligent. After the war, he worked as a laborer at the McWayne Cast Iron Pipe Company in Birmingham. Like most fathers, he wanted the best for his family. But it was not easy for Black Americans in the South during the time before the Civil Rights Movement. While working as a laborer, he used his GI status to take classes at night at Booker T. Washington Business College, which was established in the late 1930s for Black Americans by A. G. Gaston, who was one of the most successful Black businessmen in Birmingham and the United States. After completing his training in business administration, my dad passed the civil service exam which landed him a job with the federal government in Washington, DC. Initially, the job was temporary, so my dad did not move the family when he left the South.

My mother stayed in Birmingham to care for my sister and me until my dad's job situation was permanent. She was considered fortunate that she did not have to work outside of the home. However, she did alterations and baking for other people to help support the household. Some of her customers were White people. She had a sweet spiritual nature, was not overly religious, and was often very strict. The serious part of her nature often made the house unbearable for me because I was happy-go-lucky and loved listening to jazz and classical music that helped me master my dance moves. I believe she feared the Lord and respected his power. During stormy weather, one of her favorite sayings was "Fear the Lord your God with all your heart." She would make us sit quietly until the storm passed. There were times when I thought that God was going to punish me for not always being serious-minded. I believe my mother's stern hand was based on the promise that she made to my dad that she would not allow any harm to come our way until he was able to get the family together again in one place. When my dad left Birmingham to pursue work in Washington, DC, I was just a baby. But I felt the void of his presence in the house. My mother had to be a brave woman to carry on the household by herself with two young children. Thank God, we had other family members living in Birmingham who were there to help look out for us, in addition to a loving community where the neighbors looked out for each other as well.

The community where we lived was located on the west side of downtown Birmingham. Our street is located between Fifteenth and Sixteenth Streets at Second Avenue just two blocks from Third Avenue West, the main route into downtown Birmingham. Our house, like every other house on the street, had the same floor plan with a nice-sized front yard and a large backyard. Our street in the neighborhood at that time was an unpaved graveled dead-end street with an open ditch that separated us from the White neighbors at Sixteenth Street and Second Avenue West. We had beautiful green grass in our yards, and all the neighbors kept their yards neat and well-trimmed. Our front yard had a nice big shade treat at that time. The streets and avenues were paved with sidewalks in the other section of the community. The community was referred to as Rising

West Princeton. The Black part of the community consisted of a mixture of backgrounds. The neighborhood included schoolteachers, school principals, nurses, mechanics, laborers, general contractors, and storefront owners.

The west side of downtown Birmingham seemed to me at that time isolated from the rest of Birmingham. Everything usually happened on the north or south side of Birmingham. The west side was always quiet except in the springtime on Saturday and Sunday evenings when we would hear the sounds of the race cars speeding around the track at the Fair Park Motor Speedway five blocks to the west of our community. The sound was so loud that it seemed as if the cars were right in our backyard. We only had the privilege of hearing the race cars speed around the track because only Whites could attend the races. An amusement park was connected to the motor speedway park that was for "Whites only" as well. We could hear the sounds of excitement and pleasure but did not have the privilege of experiencing the excitement. As a young child, I could not fully grasp the reason I could not go to the amusement park and ride on the merry-go-round and the other rides in the park when it opened every spring right before Easter.

My parents tried their best to shield us from the dark side of racism while we were younger; but the ugly truth, racism, was everywhere. Jim Crow laws barred us from local and state public facilities. The "separate but equal" doctrine formed the basis for discrimination in public schools, public restrooms, theaters, public transportation, down to the water fountains. The sting and pain of the Jim Crow laws were only felt when we left the confines of our little community. We were "separate but definitely not equal" in every aspect of the laws.

I remember the years from 1954 to 1968 were known in the United States and especially Birmingham, Alabama, as the years of the Civil Rights Movement that brought an end to some of the visible signs of the Jim Crow era. I attended Princeton Elementary School, which was built in the early 1950s, which was right up the street from my house. In spite of the 1954 Supreme Court ban on segregation in public schools in the Brown vs. Board of Education decision, all the children at Princeton Elementary School were "Colored." Even though White children lived less than a half-block away from the school, they traveled several miles to attend the "White only" Fairview Elementary School. Southern Whites were still practicing the Jim Crow laws of legal separation of Whites and Blacks in all public places, in spite of the Supreme Court ban on segregation in public schools.

I remember those years as being extremely tense years filled with overt hatred toward Black Americans and most White Americans resisting the change. During the time before the bus boycott in 1955, Colored people were not allowed to walk past the White people on the bus. The bus driver would open the front door of the bus, step to the door, collect the fare, and then allow you to walk to the back door of the bus to get on and sit or stand behind the sign that had "Colored" on the back and "White" on the front. Usually, the seats available for Coloreds were behind the exit door. When there were more Blacks on the bus than Whites, the bus driver would not move the sign to make room for the Blacks even though there were empty seats in front of the sign in the White section of the bus. If too many Blacks were waiting at the bus stop, that was reason enough for the bus driver not to stop at that bus stop. To me, riding public transportation was a humiliating and degrading experience to endure. And to me as a young child, sometimes it was a scary event. Before my father left to work in Washington, DC, my family didn't have to use public transportation. Dad was fortunate enough to own a Black 1945 Chevrolet four-door sedan. My mother did not know how to drive, so when Dad left to work in Washington, DC, he parked the car in the backyard. While Dad was away, our only means of transportation to church and downtown was the city bus system, or occasionally, we would use the taxi service. And on special occasions, relatives and close friends would provide us with transportation to our destinations.

In 1955, I was seven years old when Rosa Parks was arrested for refusing to give up her seat to a White person in Montgomery, Alabama. That event really escalated my fear of riding the public bus. During the bus boycott period, I felt a sense of relief not having to walk two blocks from our house to the bus stop at Fifteenth Street and Third Avenue West. Walking to the bus stop meant walking one block past the area where the White people lived. When we got to that point, we had to walk in the street because we could not walk on the White people's sidewalk. I remember the times when our mother would hold our hands very tightly and tell us to stay close together until we reached the bus stop. When race relations in Birmingham were at their worst, White people would try to run you off the road just for the fun of it or because they felt their privileged status allowed them to do whatever they wanted to do and sometimes throw trash at you from their vehicle. And to make matters even worse, when you got to the bus stop, there was no guarantee that the bus driver would stop and let you get on the bus. For me, that was a humiliating experience that left scars in my memory about riding the city bus even today.

While the bus boycott was in process, the Black communities rallied together to form carpools and private bus services with small vans and trucks. Fortunately, our neighborhood was a close-knit group of people who especially looked out for those neighbors who depended on the city bus for transportation. When the Supreme Court ruled on November 14, 1956, that the segregation law in Alabama on public transportation was unconstitutional, the power of the bus boycott was a milestone toward improving some of the race relations in the South.

I was eight years old when this law was passed. I remember seeing the joy on my mother's face. I never understood why Mother did not learn how to drive the car that was just sitting in the backyard. I often thought, if Mother could drive, we would not have had to face the humiliation of riding on the city bus. Even after the Supreme Court ruled segregation on public transportation unconstitutional, I was not excited about riding the city bus again. But at least my sister and I did not have to stand and watch Mother pay the fare and then walk to the back door of the bus to get on anymore. After we got the privilege to sit wherever we wanted to on the bus, I felt empowered to sit in the seat right behind the bus driver. Mother was not always happy with me choosing that seating position when available, but I couldn't get the image of going to the back door of the bus to get on out of my head. So the front-seat experience made me feel like I was somebody special like Rosa Parks.

Throughout the midfifties and midsixties, my family lived between Birmingham, Alabama, and Washington, DC. While my dad continued to work in Washington, DC, my mother, my sister, and I resided in Birmingham from September to May; and from June to August, we would all reside together in Washington, DC. My dad would come back to Birmingham for the Thanksgiving and Christmas holidays. I thought that the living arrangement was a little strange. I personally preferred the living experience while we were in DC. My parents never explained the reason behind that living arrangement. But apparently, it worked for them until my dad retired. However, I had a strong dislike for the Birmingham experience where we spent most of our living time.

The times we spent in DC were times to escape the racial discrimination in the South. The friends whom I met in DC all thought my sister Ann and I were special "Colored" children because we were able to leave the South during the summer and not have to work in the cotton fields. We tried to explain that Birmingham is a big city somewhat like Washington, DC. I'm guessing the image in their minds about the Southland was all cotton fields and farmlands. Sometimes, they teased my sister and me about our Southern accent. But I felt that my sister and I had the upper hand on our DC friends. We had the experience and exposure to both the Southern and Eastern life experiences. We also had the opportunity to travel to New York every other summer while we were in DC, to visit our mother's sister, Aunt Mary, and our mother's mother, whom we called Nana. Aunt Mary had two girls, Amener and Isha. Amener is two years younger than I, and Isha is two years younger than her sister. We had a close bond as first cousins. They came to visit us in DC during summers when we didn't go to New York.

On our travel to the East, I did feel a little special when we rode the Silver Comet, a streamlined passenger train, from Birmingham, Alabama, to Washington, DC, each summer. But before the Supreme Court ruling in 1956 outlawed segregation on public transportation, the Birmingham Terminal Station had a small waiting area for "Coloreds." Also, there was a separate passenger car on the train designated for "Coloreds." I remember that we were not allowed to sit or eat in the dining car until the train left the Southern states. When the train was rolling through the Southern states, we could only go to the door of the dining car and purchase snacks to take back to the "Colored" passenger car. To avoid having us feel humiliated and see the White people stare at us like we were not supposed to be there, Mother packed a lunch for us when we traveled. On the occasions when Mother didn't pack snacks for us, we had to walk through the passenger cars where the White people were riding to get to the dining car. The little White children would look and point their fingers at us and say, "Look at the niggers." My heart would ache. Being called a name that carried an ugly stigma by White Americans just because my skin color was not the same as theirs was hurtful and degrading. My mother's brave spirit always told us to hold our heads up and ignore them because they did not know any better. That's what their parents taught them to call us, or they probably heard their parents refer to us using that word. Even though I felt humiliation being referred to by the word, I tried not to let the word *nigger* affect how I felt about myself. I believed that I was a child of God, and nowhere in the Bible can that word be found. However, *Webster's* dictionary describes the term as a slang and contemptuous term used to refer to a Black person. I did resent the fact that the White people rode in the front passenger cars and the Black passenger cars were almost at the end of the train. Similar to the public bus experience. Once we arrived in Washington, DC, the atmosphere and the attitudes of the White people were totally different from the attitudes in the South. However, in the early sixties, Washington, DC, had its own discrimination issues but not like in the South. The cultural experience I gained from my time in Washington, DC, helped to ease some of the pain of the racial barriers I experienced living in Birmingham, Alabama.

The first time I remember seeing the White House, the capital, the Lincoln Memorial, the Smithsonian Institute, and the Washington

Monument was in 1954. I was excited as a young child to see such elegant buildings. I marveled at their beauty. The experience of touring the capital, the Lincoln Memorial, the Library of Congress, the Smithsonian Museum, and the Washington Monument will always be in my memory. I especially remember the times when we would have picnics on the Washington Monument grounds on the Fourth of July while waiting to see the fireworks display when the sun went down. The beauty of the Fourth of July experiences was seeing people of different ethnic backgrounds enjoying the celebration of that day in peace and harmony together.

Returning to the South at the beginning of September each year was always a sad time for me and my sister. I am sure it was painful and sad for my parents as well, but they always put on their brave faces in front of us. I am sure God had to be in the center of their relationship for them to be able to endure the distance apart for such long periods. I did not understand why my family had to reside in two separate cities. I really hated going back to Birmingham. The place that made me feel unsafe and invisible. Our DC friends hated to see us leave as well. Once back in Birmingham, the sense of freedom diminished, and the underlying fear of racism was once again before me. When I reached my teen years, the adjustment back to Southern life was much harder than when I was younger. I was old enough to feel and understand the pain and burden of segregation in the city of Birmingham.

When the protest actions began in the spring of 1962 to boycott Birmingham's downtown businesses, I was fourteen and at the end of my first year in high school. The protesters were the Black students from the local Black colleges, Miles, and Daniel Payne (1889–1979); and it was led by Reverend Fred Shuttleworth. The student protestors patrolled the downtown area to make sure Blacks were not patronizing stores that promoted and tolerated segregation. The campaign was known as the Selective Buying Campaign supported by the Alabama Christian Movement for Humans Rights (ACMHR). The boycott caused a significant decline in the downtown businesses. So much so that the president of the Chamber of Commerce, Sidney Smyer, recognized that segregation was bad for business and, if Birmingham did not change, it would die. Smyer said that he was still a segregationist but that he was not a fool, and he recognized that racial unrest was damaging Birmingham businesses.

The Birmingham Board of Education decided to punish the high school student protesters who were seniors by expelling them from school and not allowing them to graduate with their classmates. However, the board did allow the suspended students to attend summer school to make up the time. The punishment also included making it difficult for me and the Black students who lived on the West side of town to get to school on the north side. For those of us whose parents were not able to drive us to school—which was the majority of us, the city bus system was our only means to get to Parker High School on the north side of town. The Birmingham School Board did not provide transportation for the Black students to get to their designated schools. There were days when the city bus driver would not stop and let us on the bus when too many of us were standing at the bus stop. When the bus driver did stop, we rode the bus from the west side into downtown Birmingham and got a transfer ticket to ride another bus to get to school on the north side. On those days when the bus did not stop, we had to walk about four miles to get to school, which meant we would be late and exhausted by the time we arrived. Our principal, R. C. Johnson, understood the circumstances and did not punish us for being tardy. Those events did not break our spirit. We walked together in groups and sang songs along the way. Singing songs along the way made the distance seem shorter. It was hard for me to grasp how adult White people could be so mean toward young teenagers who were on their way to school to get an education. It was bad enough that we could not go to the public high school closer to our neighborhood. Now remember this is the time after the 1954 Supreme Court banned segregation in public schools in the Brown vs. Board of Education decision. In spite of the barriers and optical in place to make the move forward difficult, I held onto hope for a better future.

The boycott of Birmingham businesses continued into the spring of 1963. The mass meeting organized by Martin Luther King Jr. and the SCLC was held at Sixteenth Street Baptist Church to accommodate a large number of participants. The meetings were held to train and empower the morale of the participants and recruit volunteers who would be willing to go to jail. The boycott intensified the week before Easter—the second busiest shopping season of the year—when pastors urged their congregations to avoid shopping in Birmingham stores in the downtown district. Our pastor, Rev. John H. Cross, also encouraged the congregation not to wear the usual Easter attire on Easter Sunday in support of the protest.

As a high school student, I felt helpless but hopeful for the cause. I did not want to go to jail, but I was willing to go. Although, my mother had warned my sister and me to stay away from the mass meetings at the church because she feared for our lives. In spite of her warnings, we secretly attended one of the meetings after school when the organizers began recruiting students from the local high schools to take part in the demonstrations.

After Martin Luther King Jr. was arrested on a Good Friday, April 12, 1963, along with some Birmingham leaders from the Alabama Christian Movement for Human Rights, the eyes of the nation were on Birmingham. The mayor at that time, Albert Boutwell, referred to Martin Luther King Jr. and the Southern Christian Leadership Conference organizers as "outsiders" whose only purpose in Birmingham was to stir up racial discord, even though racial harmony between Whites and Blacks did not exist for the most part. Even harmony amongst the White political leaders was at a discord. Birmingham had two city governments attempting to conduct business. The former mayor, Eugene "Bull" Connor, refused to accept the new mayor's authority after he lost the race for mayor in November 1962. Serving as public safety commissioner, Bull Connor made a promise to fill the jail with as many protesters who were violating the Jim Crow laws as long as he was at city hall.

During that Good Friday, while Martin Luther King Jr. was confined in the Birmingham City jail, he wrote a very long letter to his fellow clergymen explaining why he came to Birmingham. As president of the Southern Christian Leadership Conference, an organization operating in every Southern state, with headquarters in Atlanta, Georgia, he was asked to assist with the nonviolent direct-action program to help bring racial justice to the Black citizens in Birmingham. When the time came, King and his associates lived up to their promise. Martin Luther King Jr. stated that he could not just sit idly by in Atlanta, Georgia, and not be concerned about the injustice situation in Birmingham. King also stated in his letter that "injustice anywhere is a threat to justice everywhere." He addressed the idea of being considered an outsider. King stated that anyone who lives inside the United States can never be considered an outsider anywhere within its bounds. Looking through my lens of facts, the Jim Crow laws made me feel like an outsider, invisible, and sometimes unworthy as a citizen of Birmingham. Navigating day to day with that thought process was a heavy burden to carry and not have hate in my heart toward my enemies.

On May 2, 1963, my sister and I, along with the other students in my neighborhood, left home to go to school as usual. However, when we arrived at Parker High School that morning, we did not go on the school grounds because we had planned to join with the students who were going to take part in the protest that day. The majority of the student body had gathered together on the outside perimeter of the school building. After the remaining students inside were able to get out of the school building, we all walked to the Sixteenth Street Baptist Church to get instructions on how to march into the downtown area and conduct the sit-in at the selected businesses.

I felt empowered and afraid at the same time as we left the church in small groups singing the freedom song "We Shall Overcome." The police were prepared to arrest us but were surprised by the number of students and our nonviolent behavior. They had paddy wagons and school buses available to take us to jail. On that day, the group of students that my sister and I were with escaped being taken to jail. They put us on a school bus that took us to Fair Parks at the state fairgrounds that was used as an overflow for the city jail. They locked us behind a chained fence area that had been used to hold livestock. I guess in their minds, they thought of us as animals. However, we were released right before the sun went down. Lucky for me and my sister along with our neighbors, the state fairgrounds was within walking distance from our community. When my sister and I got home, Mother gave us a strange look. She said, "Don't tell me you all skipped school to participate in the protest." Although she had told us to stay away, she spoke in a supportive voice. So I was ready for the next phase of the protest.

The next day, when we gathered at the church and walked across the street toward Kelly Ingram Park singing the freedom song, the police warned us to turn back, or we would get wet. The first group of students went ahead in spite of the warning. When I saw what the water was doing to those students on the front line, my fear escalated to panic level. I told my sister that I did not have the courage to face the water from the fire hoses. Before we felt the sting of the water, we went back to the church to avoid the full force of the water from the fire hose. As I watched what was happening to the other protesters who continued, I was horrified when I saw the policemen allowing the dogs to charge and attack the protesters. The hatred that was displayed by the police and firemen toward Black children was an image etched in my mind and soul that I will remember forever. "How could this be happening?" As we turned back, I said to my sister and the other protesters who had turned back to avoid the force from the water hose, "This really cannot be happening. We are just God's children marching for the right to freedom, equality, and justice."

Television cameras and photographers from all around the country were there capturing the images of the violence as the dogs attacked and the force of the water from the fire hoses was being sprayed on children and teenagers. The eyes of the world were on Birmingham, Alabama, that day. Some onlookers in the area ignored the nonviolence request from the SCLC leaders and taunted the police, which made the police show even more hatred toward the protesters. Police Commissioner Eugene "Bull" Connor ordered the police to block the doors of the church to prevent those of us who stayed behind from leaving the church. We were not allowed to leave the church until the Civil Right leaders disbursed the protesters from Kelly Ingram Park, who were headed into the downtown district after the policemen decided to pull back the dogs and the firemen turned off the water hoses. The protesters who were struck by the full force of the water were badly hurt, and I learned that the dogs had badly injured some of the protesters who were on the front line of attack. It was very hard for me to comprehend what I had just witnessed. I asked myself again, "Did that really happen, or was I dreaming?" The event reminded me of the biblical time when the children of Israel who had been in bondage departed from Egypt. God sent Moses to deliver Israel, and God sent Martin Luther King Jr. to deliver Black Americans in Birmingham from the bondage of White supremacy and injustice.

By the third day of the protest, the situation in downtown Birmingham had reached a crisis stage. No business of any kind was being conducted. The jails were filled to capacity. Commissioner Bull Connor transformed the stockade at the state fairgrounds where we had been taken the day before into a makeshift jail to hold the protesters. Alabama's governor George Wallace at that time sent Alabama State troopers to Birmingham to assist Commissioner Connor with the protesters in addition to having the Alabama National Guard on standby when a large group of protestors invaded downtown Birmingham to stage sit-ins at the lunch counters. The local college students were trained to carry out the sit-in demonstrations.

My sister and I took heed to our mother's earlier warning to stay away from the downtown protest because we didn't want to risk getting expelled from school. So my sister and I, along with most of the students from our neighborhood, remained in school for the remainder of the protest period instead of meeting at the church with the other students who invaded the downtown streets, sidewalks, stores, and city buildings. However, after school, those of us from the west side of Birmingham rode the city bus that would take us through downtown to get home. Once we reached the downtown area, we joined the protest with the other students who were holding picket signs and singing freedom songs. The police did not arrest the protesters with the picket signs walking the streets. They arrested the protestors who were staging the sit-in at the lunch counters attempting to drink from the "Whites only" water fountains and those attempting to use the designated "Whites only" restrooms.

After days of protests, the White business leaders decided to agree to most of the demands that the Civil Rights leaders were requesting. The city of Birmingham agreed to desegregate the lunch counters, restrooms, drinking fountains, and fitting rooms, and to hire Blacks as sales clerks in the department stores. Before the demands, Black people were hired to do only custodian work and operate the elevators. Operating the elevator was a step above being a custodian. Behind the scene, some Blacks were hired to do tailoring and alterations in the major department stores.

The agreement to meet the demands of the Civil Rights leaders was to take place within ninety days from the date May 15, 1963. Commissioner Bull Connor was not happy with the resolution made by the city officials. The next day after the city of Birmingham had agreed to most of the demands, a bomb damaged the front portion of the Gaston Motel, where Martin Luther King Jr. and his associates had been staying during the protest. Another bomb damaged the home of A. D. King, Martin Luther King's brother. A. D. King had been arrested and jailed on a Palm Sunday for parading without a permit at Birmingham City Hall. Those events led to several hours of rocks and bottles thrown at the police who came to investigate the scenes in the areas that had been bombed which they were probably aware of even before the bombings occurred. The situation also led to federal troops coming to Birmingham to help restore order. Thank God! No one was killed or injured from the destruction of the bombs. Martin Luther King Jr. and his supporters had left the motel just hours before the bomb damaged the front portion of the motel. That's when I realized that there had to be someone else greater than man in control of what was going on. After Dr. King heard what happened, he returned to Birmingham to stress to the protesters that they should continue the nonviolent process. Throughout the campaign and protest, Dr. King always stressed nonviolence. However, through my eyes, I saw the hatred and violence coming from the hearts and minds of the people who were anti-justice and anti-equality for all.

By the end of May, some calm seemed to surround the city. The newly elected mayor, Albert Boutwell, was allowed to take office after the Alabama Supreme Court ruled outgoing Mayor Art Hanes could no longer hold the position. The city of Birmingham had been at an impasse after Hanes served just one term as major. He refused to give up the position even after the citizens voted him out. Police Commissioner Eugene "Bull" Connor was Hanes's right-hand man. They were part of a three-man commission that ran the city during the tumultuous time when the Birmingham campaign was burgeoning. Certainly, that was not a good example of how the city government was supposed to function according to what I learned in my civics education class.

Moving beyond that perilous time, the school year ended on a good note. I made the honor roll as usual. I was selected to be one of the three head cheerleaders on the cheering squad. I was voted to be on the student government board, and I joined the Future Teachers of America Club. Not that I wanted to be a teacher. But as a member of the Future Teachers of America Club, you had the privilege of serving as a teacher during American Education Week in the subject area that you considered your best. My strongest areas were mathematics and science. My future looked somewhat hopeful, even inside the Southern region of the United States, where racism, hatred, and the Jim Crow laws still lingered in spite of the civil rights demands and the agreements made by the city officials.

Once again, it was time to return to Washington, DC, for the summer after the school year had come to an end. I was both happy and sad about going to DC in the summer of 1963. On one hand, I was happy to be able to get away from the evils of racism in the South but sad that I would not be around to witness the results of the agreements made by the city officials to meet the demands made by Dr. King and the Alabama Christian Movement for Human Rights. However, I needed to relieve my mind from the anxiety, fear, and doubt brought on by all the protesting. I needed to be filled with new energy and strength to take the next steps in my life. I used to hear my mother say all the time that "You have to give all your worries and cares to God that you have no control over and let him take care of them." I really did not understand how to comprehend that idea at fifteen years old.

Taking ballet and modern dance lessons, going to school, and church were the highlights of my life. Those activities gave me purpose and kept me grounded. I was taught to always do what was right and good. I often wondered if some White Americans felt that they were exempt from doing what is right and good. If so, that meant they didn't have a soul. Anyone who could drape a cross with White cloth—the cross that represents Christ's suffering and death for our sins so that we could be free—and then set it on fire cannot have a heart for Christ. The hatred that was shown by Bull Connor when he ordered the police to use attack dogs and the firemen to use their fire hoses to control young children who were nonviolent protesters marching for justice and freedom reminds me of the time when Jesus was brought before Pontius Pilate to be sentenced to death even though there were no grounds for crucifying Jesus. Then Pilate's soldiers were allowed to scourge and dehumanize Jesus before he was placed on the Cross to die. For the police and firemen to execute such a cruel and inhumane act toward young innocent children, their souls had to be sick or dead. But it had to be God's grace and mercy that prevented anyone from dying during those traumatic events.

I tried very hard not to allow my thoughts to linger on the events that happened, but it was very difficult not to. As difficult as times were in the South during the sixties, I am so grateful that Martin Luther King Jr. and his followers felt obligated and compelled to engage in any efforts to help bring about justice and freedom, not only for Black Americans in Birmingham, Alabama, but for people all over the world who were being deprived of their human rights. The ugly truth about the injustice of the Jim Crow laws that had been imposed on the lives of Black Americans in Birmingham, Alabama, and all over the Southern parts of the United States was surreal. In spite of the ugly truth about racism and segregation, Black Americans somehow had the spirit of hope within. Through the spirit of hope, I felt some sense of freedom. Freedom to have high hopes and dreams for the future to live the best life possible with limitless possibilities. With that thought process, I believe that freedom is a state of mind, not a tangible condition.

Freedom, equality, and justice for Black Americans came with a high price tag. Our Creator created human life out of love. His purpose for human life here on earth is for us to be free to experience the joys of life without repression to do his will. However, White supremacists believed that idea was only good for White Americans. We are all fearfully and wonderfully made to coexist on a tiny planet that resides in a small section of a rather insignificant solar system. Our earth, in reality, is just one minuscule blue dot among millions of celestial bodies that God created. Our Creator singled out each person on this planet as supremely important. But Southern White supremacists created laws to make Black Americans unimportant, insufficient, and powerless.

The ugly truth about White supremacists' ideals is that they wanted Black Americans to believe that we were not worthy to play the game of life. With God's power and wisdom and through the leadership of our civil rights leaders, Black Americans in Birmingham, Alabama, and other parts of the Southland were able to see the foul and unfair play presented by White supremacy and decided to call it out. Black Americans decided to move beyond the mind-set of feeling powerless. I had to find a place of forgiveness within me in order to deal with the very painful memories of the ugly events that happened that are etched into the memory of my mind forever. But in my heart, I felt that I must forgive the ugly truth of the Jim Crow laws to free myself from the atrocities committed against my soul, mind, and heart.

The truth is! How do I forget?

I believe in truth with a capital *T*. My belief in *truth* is what firmly upholds me. When I was very young, my parents always told me to tell the truth. They constantly reminded me and my sister that the truth is the same yesterday, today, tomorrow, and forever. Throughout my life, I have always been compelled to speak the truth. Whenever I was tempted to speak the untruth, my parents' voice would echo in my head, and I would stop myself.

The ugly truth regarding the Jim Crow laws should be changed. The Jim Crow laws were never true, honorable, and just laws. The laws were not pure, loving, or good. Forgiving the ugly truth will be a long and forever process for me each and every day of my life. Each day that I have breath, I will need to fill my whole consciousness with the *spirit of real truth* to help me continue to forgive.

Chapter 2

I always thought that summertime should be a time to let go and be free to have fun and enjoy the pleasures of life—especially in the city where the US capital is located, where there are neoclassical monuments and buildings and iconic museums to visit. But the summer of 1963, my mind was consumed with thoughts about the leaders of the city of Birmingham not following through with the terms of the arrangements that were agreed upon to desegregate the city. Having thoughts of going back to the same status quo of the Jim Crow laws was very troubling to my mind and heart. I felt like I was invisible. I was not in the position to do anything but pray. The small role that I played in the protest was empowering. The experience of participating in the protest left me with unsettling feelings. Flashbacks of images of the water from the fire hoses and the dogs attacking the protesters continued to dominate my thoughts. The images were burned in my mind. I had trouble sleeping. Thoughts of what life could be like living in the city of Birmingham without the barriers of racism flooded my mind. Thoughts of how wonderful it would be if peace and harmony existed between the races. My thoughts were so conflicted and clouded with doubt that I could not see the future as a smiling face.

This was the first summer that I was not excited about leaving Birmingham to go to Washington, DC. I wanted to stay in Birmingham to witness the changes that were supposed to take place.

But I had no choice in the matter. The burden of racism was a heavy burden to bear. Fears concerning what the future holds for me were scary. It was difficult expressing these feelings to my parents. They did not openly show their concerns about the unfair way of life. We never discussed the topic as a family. But, on the other hand, when I had my father-daughter moments, he told me that some Southern White men are incorrigible "devils." He told me to always keep my eyes open and be aware of the wicked. My sister and I had different views regarding racism when we discussed history. I pointed out that information about Black Americans' culture was missing from the pages of the history textbooks. That didn't seem to matter to her. She only seemed to be concerned with just remembering the information presented to get her A out of the course. But I had a deep burning in my soul to do something to help bring about change but didn't exactly know-how at that point in my life. In the early sixties, I wished I could have been on the front line with the Freedom Riders and the Student Nonviolence Coordinating Committee (SNNC), who were seeking to see our nation become what it should be—the land of the free. I believe that America could actually become a democracy for all the people. My heart and mind knew that it was unjust for Southern Whites to treat Black Americans like we were not human. I could not understand their need to be so mean and full of hate toward another human simply because of skin color. I often wondered if they knew the same Jesus that my parents taught me about and I learned about when I read the Bible and heard my Sunday school teachers talked about and the minister preached about.

I was taught to live my best life and seek my highest potential. But I didn't always know how to go about doing so with the barriers and restrictions before me. I was taught to be patient and wait for my blessings. But at that time, it was hard to look toward the future and see a path forward that included people like me. I prayed every day that life would be better for Black Americans in the city of Birmingham. When Martin Luther King Jr. was confined in the Birmingham city jail, I am pretty sure he had to seek divine wisdom within to give him the insight and directions needed to carry out a positive course of action with the nonviolent movement to help change the racial injustice engulfing the most thoroughly segregated city in the United States.

While I was patiently waiting for the summer to end, I kept up with the news regarding the small changes that were taking place in Birmingham. I was eagerly waiting to hear that the signs displaying "Whites only" and "Colored" had been removed from public view, especially on the city bus and the water fountains. Like Martin Luther King Jr. expressed in his letter from the Birmingham jail, I, too, found it very difficult to wait. My cup of endurance had overflowed. I was tired of feeling tense and anxious. I wanted to feel the same kind of freedom living in Birmingham, Alabama, like the freedom I felt during my summer vacations in Washington, DC. I was taught to believe that freedom is a blessing that we all inherited as children of God. Yet nearly one hundred years after the Emancipation Proclamation, Black Americans in Birmingham, Alabama, and other Southern states lived in an unequal world of disenfranchisement, segregation, and various forms of oppression. I needed to believe that the results from the protest would give me the opportunity to experience some of the blessings that the Creator has so generously provided for mankind on this earth.

The Birmingham protest was a clear indication that Black Americans were determined to seek justice and equality at any cost. Black Americans were no longer willing to accept racial segregation on any level. I was taught to be a believer and to trust that my future would be secure and not be controlled by external circumstances or other individuals—which gave me the faith to believe that Birmingham and the other Southern states would be a better place to live one day. I knew that the walls of segregation and discrimination were not going to come down overnight, but I knew it had to happen even though some forces were trying to block the change. The small part I played in the protest gave me a new sense of dignity and self-respect. My faith has taught me to believe that God loves all of his children and that I was created in his image to have the freedom to make choices and seek greater meaning and fulfillment in life without fear. I was also taught to believe that I am a precious gift from God and I am worthy of the many blessings of life. Yet the Jim Crow laws made me feel that the reality of these blessings was not possible. But as a protester, although not on the front line getting attacked by vicious dogs, enduring the water pressure from the fire hoses, and escaping going to jail, I was infused with courage and steadfastness to march to help bring about change.

By the end of July 1963, I learned that most of the segregation ordinances in the city of Birmingham had been overturned. The Jim Crow signs regulating segregation in public places were taken down. Some of the lunch counters in department stores complied with the new rules. Public parks and entertainment centers were opened to Black citizens with certain restrictions. But the hiring of Blacks as clerks in stores, police officers, and firefighters had not yet complied with the desegregation ordinances. In spite of the small changes, it was hard for me to believe that the Southern states and the Northeastern states are part of the same United States of America. The Constitution of the United States of America that we were required to learn about in high school and remember affirms that justice and domestic tranquility, common defense, general welfare, and the blessing of liberty and posterity are for all the people of the United States. Or was it for all the people? In my heart, I believed the words of the Constitution, but through my eyes, the Constitution was not protecting all the people. I felt that my general welfare was not worthy of promoting and protecting. But the power of the nonviolent protest exposed the moral defenses of most Southern White Americans and began to weaken their morality. When I think about how we, the protesters, marched for justice without stooping to violence and hatred in the process, I knew there had to be some divine order of power working through us.

During my previous summers in Washington, DC, I did not realize until after I experienced the 1963 protest in Birmingham that racial injustice was a national problem. Washington, DC, had subtle and hidden forms of racial injustice. The injustice exists in the areas of employment discrimination, housing discrimination, and school discrimination. My father was a computer program analyst with the federal government in the Veterans Administration Division. He was the only Black in his department during that time. I didn't think of it as racial injustice until I learned otherwise. I was just glad that my father was employed and earned enough money to take care of the family. When I think back, I realize now that Shepherd Street, Northwest, Washington, DC, where my father resided consisted of all Black Americans except for the storefront business owned by foreigners and run by Black Americans, which was a clear indication of housing and employment discrimination. The few friends that I made while spending summers in DC all attended all-Black schools. But having access to public transportation, public parks and museums, and other governmental monuments without barriers, you didn't think about the subtle and hidden racial injustices that were in existence. These facts were called to my conscience and thousands of other Black Americans when Martin Luther King Jr. addressed them in his speech at the Great March on Detroit, June 1963.

In June 1963, another historical moment came to my conscience regarding the Declaration of Independence, which we were required to learn about in my high school American history class. The document was adopted by the Continental Congress on July 4, 1776, declaring the thirteen American colonies as independent states from the British Empire to form a new nation—the United States of America. A portion of the Declaration expresses a fundamental view regarding human rights that all humans are created equal and our Creator gave us certain inalienable rights such as life, liberty, and the pursuit of happiness. That portion of the Declaration came to represent a moral standard which the United States should strive to follow.

The state of Alabama was admitted to the union of the new nation on December 14, 1819, which meant that as a state in the United States, Alabama should also strive to follow these moral standards that are revealed in the Declaration of Independence. Yet in 1963, the officials of the city of Birmingham, the largest city in the state of Alabama, did not honor and respect the Declaration of Independence or the Constitution of the United States of America in relation to Black Americans. The idea behind the Declaration of

Independence is that all people are born into a free world with certain rights that cannot be taken away by anyone. But in Birmingham, Alabama, the human rights of Black Americans were being violated, and justice was not in our favor. The form of government instituted in the city of Birmingham affected the safety and happiness of Black American citizens. The Constitution states that it is the right of the people to alter or abolish that form of government and institute a new government that would recognize the human rights of all the people. The Birmingham protest which attracted media attention to the adverse treatment of Black Americans caused national forces to take interest in the issues of justice and human rights. The Birmingham protest was a means to abolish the old form of government that excluded the rights of Black Americans and institute a new government that created safety and happiness for all humans.

In August 1963, when I learned that Martin Luther King Jr. and the SCLC leaders were planning the March on Washington for jobs and freedom, my mind immediately took me back to the protest that I experienced in May in Birmingham. On one hand, I felt fortunate to already be in Washington, DC, so that I could participate. But at the same time, fear struck my heart because of what I witnessed in Birmingham. According to the news media, people all over America felt fear in their hearts regarding the idea of masses of Black Americans marching on Washington, DC. Looking back to 1928, before I was born, I can imagine when the Ku Klux Klan paraded down Pennsylvania Avenue in all their hooded regalia at the zenith of their power, Black Americans had fear in their hearts. However, the leaders of the SCLC Movement confirmed that the actions of the protestors would be peaceful in spite of the negative threats that were being projected by the media. I did not understand the concern regarding the march because the marchers in Birmingham were nonviolent. The violence was perpetrated by law enforcement individuals who were supposed to protect and serve the citizens.

On the day of the march, Washington, DC, took actions to limit public transportation to get to the Lincoln Memorial. But my sister, my DC friends, and I were determined to take part in the march.

We were determined to take part in a history-making moment. So we walked from Shepherd Street, Northwest, to the reflection pool at the Lincoln Memorial. When we reached the area, we could not believe the masses of people that were there. There were just as many Whites and other races in the crowd as Blacks. There was a beautiful rainbow of people from all over the country who came to bear witness. As I stood and listened to the speakers who spoke before Martin Luther King Jr. delivered his "I Have a Dream" speech, the crowd was warm and receptive. But when King took the stand, the applause from the crowd was overwhelming. I, along with everyone in the area where my sister and my DC friends were standing, was mesmerized by the elegant and spiritual nature of his words. It was amazing to see how God was using Martin Luther King Jr. to accomplish the transformation of hearts through the life of this spiritual man and his followers. Martin Luther King's message resonated to America a call for freedom and justice for all and the necessity for change and hope in American society. When we all joined hands and sang "We Shall Overcome," I felt the spirit of love and peace flowing through the masses. People were crying and smiling at the same time. The March on Washington was a powerful march that demonstrated to the world that Black Americans would no longer accept being second-class citizens. We are citizens of this nation with certain inalienable rights!

After the march, I felt a renewed spirit of hope for change to come. For the first time in my teen years, I had hope that my future goals and dreams had a chance to be accomplished. Dreaming was one of my favorite pastimes. I considered my dreams to be a vision of something that is yet to be. I had a vision in my head of what our lives as Black Americans and the world would look like if racism did not exist. Just as Martin Luther King Jr. indicated in his "I Have a Dream" speech that one day all God's children whether Black or White will be able to join hands together as sisters and brothers. Those were powerful words. The entire speech resonated words of power that had to transform the minds and hearts of those who heard. Even though I was just a spectator in the crowd, I knew in my heart that my presence there was by the grace of God. I learned from that experience that every one of us on this earth is essential and no matter what part we play, big or small, it will make a difference in the transformation of the world.

With a renewed spirit of hope for change to come, I was ready to get back to Birmingham and face the challenges ahead. My hope for peace and harmony between the races seemed possible. With hope for the future, I would be able to put the protest images behind me of the dogs attacking and the force of the water from the fire hoses knocking humans to the ground like they were trash being washed away. Although I was not directly attacked by the dogs or knocked down by the force of the water, I had a sense of the agony and pain that the protesters must have felt. But I felt blessed by those protesters who put their lives on the front line so that Black Americans would one day be free from the bondage of segregation. I often wonder what was going through the minds of those policemen and firemen who were carrying out the orders of Commissioner Bull Connor. Did they have a conscience? Did they have children? If so, I wonder what they felt! I wonder! Did they feel any pain or remorse when they saw what the police and firemen were doing to innocent human beings?

At the end of August 1963, it was time for my mother, my sister, baby brother, and me to return to Birmingham before the start of the 1963 school year. Schools in the South usually open after the Labor Day holiday. I had mixed emotions about returning. But I had to go back to complete my high school education. My baby brother Edmond Junior was a surprise to my parents because I turned fifteen years old in April 1963 two months after his birth in February. That was the beginning of my junior year in high school and Ann, a senior in high school. She planned to attend Clark College, now Clark Atlanta University in Atlanta, Georgia, that following August 1964. Nevertheless, he was a blessing to the family. Thank God he was not old enough to feel the pain and hurt of racism that my sister and I were experiencing. It was my hope that by the time he reached the age to enter school, the dream that all men were free would actually come true.

As we made the journey back to the South on the Silver Comet train, I was surprised that there were no more separate passenger cars for Blacks only. We were able to ride in the same passenger cars with the White people. We were also able to eat in the dining car with the White people, but the last few tables at the very back were reserved for Blacks. I guess it's safe to say, President John F. Kennedy's message to the nation about Civil Rights in June 1963 and the March on Washington that August brought about a few changes. Some of the outward signs of segregation seemed to be disappearing. Riding the train was an exhilarating experience. I felt blessed as I watched the beautiful scenery that was created by the Creator from the train window. No form of hatred or injustice can affect the divine order of nature. No attack dogs or water from a fire hose can change the order of nature. I could not change what happened during the protest in Birmingham, but I could try and release the hurt and pain I felt by turning within to pray so that I could be open to a new and beautiful life that awaits me and the hopeful Black Americans who resided in Birmingham.

When we arrived at the Birmingham Terminal Station, I was met with another surprise. We did not have to go through the small waiting area that was designated for Coloreds when we left to go to Washington, DC, at the end of May. That area was closed off and being used as a baggage room. I was, indeed, happy not to see the "Whites Only" and "Coloreds Only" signs visible anywhere. We were able to walk through the main lobby of the station. During the eleven years that I remember traveling to Washington, DC, this was the first time that I got to see the inside of the main lobby of the train station. I was amazed at the size and beauty. The main lobby was just as beautiful as the Washington Union Station but not as large. I felt like a bird just freed from my cage. I had a skip in my steps as I was taking in the sight. My mother and sister thought I was losing my mind because I was whirling around trying to take in the view of the station before we went outside to get the taxi cab that would take us home.

It was hard for me to believe once we got outside the terminal lobby that we had the option to choose to ride with the Black-owned taxi service or the yellow taxi service that was for the most part a "Whites only" company. I remember the times before the Birmingham protest if you needed a taxi, the yellow cab taxi service would not come to the Black neighborhoods, which meant waiting for at least an hour or more to get service with the black taxi service because they were limited in number. I suggested to Mother that we take the yellow cab. She gave me a look that I will never forget and said, "No, we are using the black taxi service just as we did when we left for DC." I was disappointed because I wanted to have the privilege of being chauffeured home by a White driver. But at the same time, I was glad she said no, because, at the back of my mind, I feared what the White taxi driver might do to us even though it was broad daylight. Desegregation had just begun to take place at the end of June when the Jim Crow signs regulating segregated public places and transportation had just been taken down. And only moderate demands had been agreed upon by the Birmingham Chamber of Commerce to overturn the segregation ordinances.

As we rode through downtown Birmingham where the protest took place during the months of April and May headed to the west side of town, images of what had taken place flashed through my mind. When I closed my eyes, the images were so vivid as if it was happening all over again. The floodwaters of fear swept over my mind. I did not let on to my mother and sister what I was feeling or thinking because I did not want them to worry about me and think I was losing my mind. I tried to relax and poised my mind to be still. Because I was taught that fear is the opposite of faith, and I was not going to let my fears control me. I had to exhale all tension and inhale peace in order to calm my thoughts and emotions.

When we finally reached the west side of town and the taxi stopped in front of our house, most of my fears and anxiety had subsided. Our closest neighbors were outside in their yards when we arrived. They welcomed us back home with hugs and cold lemonade. The air in Birmingham was very hot and dry. Our house had been closed up from the end of May until the end of August. When we entered the house, it was like walking into a hot oven. My mother left the key to the house with the next-door neighbor so that the house could be opened and aired out periodically during the summer and a couple of days before we returned. However, it was still hot and muggy. In August and September, the weather was extremely hot in Alabama. And we were not fortunate enough to have air-conditioning, but we did have a fan that oscillated to help cool the house a bit. Before we could get settled and unpacked, the telephone started ringing. Mother had contacted the phone company before we left DC, to have the phone turned back on before we arrived. My mother and sister loved talking on the phone. Their close friends who did not live in the neighborhood were calling to see if we were really back in town. While we were in DC, Mother and Ann communicated with their friends by mail. Since I considered my sister my best friend, her friends were my friends too. I had one special friend, Patricia Peters, who lived three houses from our house. Patricia and I were the same age. She was an only child and appeared to have all the necessities that she wanted. Her parents were divorced. Her mother was an elementary music school teacher, and her dad was a high school guidance counselor in the Birmingham School System. Patricia preferred to be called Pat. She played the piano very well. Sometimes, she and her mother would play duet and sing when I came to visit. Her mother had a beautiful voice. Even though Pat and I were close, we did not exchange letters throughout the summer. Pat and I also attended the same dance school. Pat was staying at her grandmother's house on the south side of Birmingham the day we returned from DC. So she was not at home on the day we returned. We eventually got together a few days before school started to exchange our experiences about the summer.

The telephone continued to ring for my mother and sister. One phone call Mother received was from one of her church friends who informed her that while we were away, the church had received several bomb threats throughout the summer. The Klan members were angry at Reverend John H. Cross for allowing Martin Luther King Jr. and the SCLC leaders to use the church to hold the mass meetings in April and May. The Klan members vowed to get Reverend Cross at any cost to teach him a lesson for letting outsiders use the church to strategize and stir up trouble from their point of view. The caller also told Mother that the church had been guarded around the clock so the members felt pretty safe about coming to church in spite of the threats. However, we did not attend church the first Sunday in September 1963 since we had just returned from DC. Mother allowed us a few days to rest before returning to school after Labor Day. But I was really looking forward to going back to church so that I could meet with my Sunday school and school classmates who attended the church to find out about all that had gone on while I was away. I wanted to learn more about the bomb threats because Mother did not give my sister and me all the details. I am pretty sure Mother was trying to keep our fear level at a minimum. The only event I was not looking forward to was riding the city bus to get to school and church.

I was surprised and happy when I learned that the Birmingham City School Board had made arrangements to provide special city buses to pick up the Black students on the west side of town and further north of Parker High School at specific locations in our areas who used the Birmingham City bus system to get to school. The White students had access to the yellow school buses provided by the board of education to get them to their designated schools. This move was made to keep public schools segregated. I always thought it was unfair and unjust that we had to pay to ride the city bus and endure the ugly treatment that we encountered to get to school and the White students had access to free transportation provided by city tax dollars. However, we still had to pay half the cost of the city bus fare to ride the *special* bus. Separate and unequal treatment. Our parents paid city tax just like the White people. The system was separate and definitely not equal. However, this move made getting to school a little more convenient for the Black students in my community since we could not attend the "White only" West End high schools closer to our homes on the west side. The *special* bus took a route that took us directly to the school campus without going through downtown Birmingham. Since White supremacists were in charge at all levels of government and had all the political power, separate and unequal practices were still in place after the movement.

Governor Wallace stood in front of the doorway of Forest Auditorium at the University of Alabama in June 1963 to block the entrance of two Black students, Vivian Malone and James A. Hood, from enrolling at the university. But Wallace had to yield when President John F. Kennedy employed his executive power and federalized National Guard troops to enforce the ruling of the 1954 Brown v. Board of Education Act. Wallace made other attempts to block the desegregation of Alabama public schools in Tuskegee, Mobile, and Huntsville. Each time Wallace made attempts to violate the law, President Kennedy employed his executive power and federalized National Guard troops to uphold the law. In spite of the actions that President Kennedy took to uphold the 1954 Brown v. Board of Education Act, Governor George Wallace was more determined to keep the city of Birmingham schools segregated regardless of the Supreme Court ruling. Governor Wallace made a vow to his White followers in his 1963 inauguration speech that in the state of Alabama, there will be "Segregation now! Segregation tomorrow! Segregation forever!" That statement had a profound impact on my mind and thoughts about continuing my education in the state of Alabama. I could not wait to graduate from high school and get out of Birmingham. Under no circumstances was I going to college anywhere in the state of Alabama. Nor did I ever consider the Black colleges in the state. I wanted to put Alabama, especially Birmingham, as far behind me as possible.

Because of Governor Wallace's rhetoric, integrating the public schools in Birmingham brought about violence. Most of the White parents were willing to close the White schools to prevent integration. They wrote letters to Governor Wallace, urging him to do anything in his power including closing schools if all else failed to prevent the integration of Birmingham public schools. Wallace ordered patrolmen to block the doors of the White schools to prevent Black students from entering. The actions of Governor Wallace clearly implied defiance of the Supreme Court's decision to integrate schools. On September 4, 1963, after Black parents made an attempt to enroll their children in the White Graymont Elementary School near their home, they later received death threats by phone if they insisted on enrolling their children. In opposition to attending school with Black students, White students protested outside West End, Ramsey and Woodlawn High Schools. The White students carried Confederate flags and signs stating, "Keep our schools White." During their protest, they were not met with dogs and water hoses. They were free to say and do as they please with no pushback.

To please his political supporters, Governor Wallace ordered the school board to close the schools that allowed Blacks to enroll. The president of the Birmingham PTA at that time rejected the call to close schools. She stated that it would be utterly impossible to put all the White students in the Birmingham school system in the private schools. In spite of the opposition by the president of the Birmingham PTA, schools closed for a week. Upon reopening, the school board allowed Black students to enroll in the school of their choice nearest their home. The White students who did not want to go to schools with the Black students boycotted classes at West End High as part of their protest. The students in my community had the option to attend West End High or continue attending Parker High. The majority of the students in my community opted to remain at Parker High. I definitely did not want to be anywhere I was not welcomed. I did not want to carry that kind of pressure and detraction on my shoulders during the school day.

Some of the White communities continued to express opposition regarding the ruling to allow Black students to enroll in the White schools. This was a true indication that most Southern Whites believed that Black Americans were not worthy of life, liberty, and pursuit of happiness. Those actions made me wonder if the Founding Fathers and the Constitution's ratifiers were referring to Black Americans when they came up with the idea of individual freedom and equality. The Constitution of the United States of America is the supreme law of the United States created to protect the fundamental rights of all United States citizens. Yet from every angle of the law, my eyes saw that Black Americans were being denied their fundamental rights according to the Constitution.

In spite of all that ugliness, I looked forward to the first day of school after summer vacation. It was a time to reunite with classmates and talk about what we experienced and learned over the summer, as well as learn which teachers would be teaching the classes that we were assigned to take for the new school year. I was on the academic track for college-bound students, which meant my class load would be full. I had reached a point in my life where I was just learning how to look beyond the apparent circumstances of bad situations and not get stuck in the negative experiences regarding what had been done and how it was done. I was learning how not to take life so personally and stay positive as I embraced each day and envisioned my future goals and aspirations while living in a city that perpetuated fear.

The tension and violence that erupted in the city of Birmingham centered around integrating schools created more fear and distrust for city leaders and police officers from the Black communities. Dozens of bombings were committed in Birmingham by unknown terrorists. Black churches, businesses, and homes of civil rights leaders were usually the targets for the explosions. The victims of these violent acts were individuals who had gone against the rigid structure of White supremacy. The Fountain Heights section, where Black families had moved into a predominately White neighborhood, was a common place for the bombings to happen. That section of town became known as "Dynamite Hill." Under the leadership of Police Commissioner Eugene "Bull" Connor, an admitted supporter of segregation, the bombing events had virtually no chance of being solved nor justice prevailing.

On September 4, 1963, the home of NAACP Attorney Arthur Shores was bombed which had been previously bombed two weeks earlier. Four days later, two fire bombs were thrown at the home of business leader A. G. Gaston. Fortunately, no one was killed by the bombs. However, fighting erupted with bricks and bottles being thrown at the police. The eruption ended when a Black man was killed by the police and dozens of other Blacks were injured and arrested. At the core of this violence was the mysterious Ku Klux Klan, who seemed to have limitless power. They were able to strike fear and violence at any time and any place. On the west side of town in my community, the atmosphere of racial hatred was not as poisoned as the Dynamite Hill area. I believed that because White families lived in homes that surrounded my community, our area was less likely to be targeted for attack. However, no one who threatened the Klan's White supremacy was safe from their hands. It was hard for me at times to comprehend how some humans could show so much hatred toward other humans because of differences in skin tone. The Klan even showed hatred toward their own race if they showed any empathy toward Blacks. The one thing that calmed my fears from thinking that the Klan might bring violence to my community was my belief that the power of God was in control of the universe. But in spite of my belief in the power of God, I was afraid to go anywhere alone even in my own neighborhood because, in Alabama, the Klan was incalculable. Their reign of terror was unabated. It was nearly impossible to get a conviction on the crimes they committed because the Klan or family members of the Klan permeated every level of governmental authority in Alabama.

Once the protesting had ended in June and most of the segregation ordinances in the city of Birmingham had been overturned and the Jim Crow signs regulating segregation in public places were taken down, I thought Birmingham was heading in the direction of peace, prosperity, and harmony for all. Desegregating the city schools seemed to dispel that idea. As I mentioned earlier, when the White community was protesting to keep their schools White, they were not faced with high-pressure water hoses and vicious dogs. They had the freedom to ride around town with signs posted on their cars "Niggers Go Home" and "Keep Birmingham Schools White" while waving their Confederate flags. Those who waved the Confederate flags were clearly expressing their belief that all men are not created equal. Waving the Confederate flag symbolized the attitude that White people wanted to continue to dehumanize Black people. Most Southern White people felt that the welfare of their children would be in jeopardy if they attended class with Black children. By the second week in September 1963, the Black students were able to attend classes at West End High School and Graymont Elementary School without any major incidents on the part of the opposing White students and their parents.

The unrest in Birmingham affected the life and welfare of everyone in the city. As a matter of fact, the city was sick. The atmosphere was poisoned with racial hatred. The city had been publicly shamed in the media by Police Commissioner Eugene "Bull" Connor when he used the fire hoses and police dogs to control the protest marchers. Even though business leaders reached an agreement that ended some of the segregation barriers, the spirit of goodwill was being overshadowed by all the violence and recent bombings. The city that was once known as the "Magic City" was now nicknamed "Bombingham." The resistance to change was ugly. It appeared to me that the city and state governments were not willing to create a city and state that works for all. However, I was not going to lose my hope for change. In my consciousness, I was willing to rise gratefully to contribute all that I could to the growth and evolution of humankind.

In spite of the unrest in the city, Sunday was a day that seemed to bring some calm to the evil deeds. Attending church was a place to go and leave the anxiety and negativity behind and think about positive things. We attended church rain or shine on Sundays. The morning of September 15, 1963, started like most Sunday mornings in our house. However, this Sunday was special. It was Youth Sunday at Sixteenth Street Baptist Church. One Sunday in each month, the pastor, Reverend John H. Cross, allowed the youth the opportunity to play the role of adults and teach the Sunday school classes and lead the worship service. On Youth Sunday in September, the girls wore white dresses, and the boys wore dark-blue or black pants and white shirts with a black tie. I was particularly excited about this Youth Sunday because I was going to help lead a song with the youth choir, and I had made myself a new white dress to wear. My sister and I were pretty good with the sewing machine during that time. Even into our adult lives. It was hard to tell that my dress was not purchased from the department store. Traditionally, in the South, you do not wear white after Labor Day. But it was Youth Sunday. After eating breakfast and putting on our white dresses, my sister and I prepared to leave the house to go to the bus stop to catch the bus. Our baby brother was still sleeping in his crib, and Mother was preparing to come to the eleven o'clock worship service. Our seven-year-old "play sister," Karen, who lived two houses from us, was going to ride the bus with us this Sunday. Ann and I considered her our sister because we were more like family than just neighbors. Karen called our mother "Ann Mama." My mother took care of her during the day while her parents were working until she reached school age. Karen's dad would drop us off at Sunday school on some Sundays and sometimes our neighbors, the Taylors, at the end of the street who attended Metropolitan AME Methodist Church two blocks from Sixteenth Street Baptist Church would also give my sister and me a ride to Sunday school on occasions. Their son Melvin and I were the same age. I considered him the brother I didn't have until Edmond was born. My next-door neighbor Robert, also the same age as Melvin and me, was like a brother as well. We were all classmates from first grade through high school graduation. Melvin had a swing that hung from a big branch on an oak tree in his backyard that we took turns swinging on. Our mothers were all very good friends. They took turns entertaining each other at each other's homes. They all had gardens in the backyard and shared their harvest.

As we made our way to the bus stop that Sunday morning, the air was warm with a slight overcast in the sky, but there was no rain in the forecast. While we waited at the bus stop for the bus to arrive, I asked my sister if she noticed the stillness in the atmosphere and how light the traffic flow was. She responded with, "There you go with your overactive imagination." Sometimes, I would have premonitions that something is about to happen. I hated having those feelings because whenever I did, something would, indeed, happen that was sometimes good and other times not so good. Once the bus arrived, we boarded and found a seat where the three of us could sit together. I noticed the bus driver looking in the rearview mirror at us. That made me feel a little uneasy. I know we had on our Sunday best. But to me, he had a look on his face as if he knew exactly which church we were going to. There was one other Black person on the bus when we got on who stayed on after we got off. Once the bus arrived at Third Avenue and Sixteenth Street North, we had to walk four more blocks to get to the church. As we were walking, my thoughts were still focused on the stillness in the atmosphere. Something just did not feel right to me. As we walked past Kelly Engram Park where the protest took place, I had flashbacks of the events that took place in May and thought about the bomb threats that had been made on the church. Once we arrived at the church, Karen went through the door that led to the basement of the church where the children ages infant to fourteen attended Sunday school. My sister and I walked up the front steps to the main sanctuary where the adolescents and adults attended Sunday school. Once we reached the section in the sanctuary where our class was sitting, we managed to sit next to each other. My classmate and friend Carolyn Maull taught the lesson that Sunday. She was very good at discerning the Word. Even though I had studied my lesson, I would not have been able to explain the lesson the way that she did.

Before the end of the lesson, I felt the need to use the restroom. I had put more liquids in my body than I should have before I left home. I told my sister that I was going downstairs to the lady's lounge. She asked why I couldn't wait until the end of the lesson. I told her that I had to go really bad. Once I reached the lounge, I saw Carol, Cynthia, Denise, and Addie standing in front of the floor-length mirror, admiring how they looked. Sara, one of Addie's older sisters, was sitting on the lounge's sofa, watching with a smile on her face. Sara was always smiling whenever I saw her. Once I used the restroom and washed my hands, I decided to take notice of myself in the mirror with the girls who were still primping. I told them that they looked beautiful. While I was looking at myself and the other girls in the wall-to-wall floor-length mirror, a loud ticking sound got my attention that was not coming from the clock on the wall. The ticking sound came from the opposite direction near a small rectangular-shaped window in the lounge on the Sixteenth Street side of the church. The window gave you only a small view of the outside. The window was overshadowed by the steps that led up to the main sanctuary. When I asked the girls if they were hearing the ticking sound, they said that they didn't hear anything. I paused and asked them to listen, but they still said that they did not hear any ticking. I was not wearing a watch, and I don't believe the other girls had on watches either. I thought maybe my mind was in overdrive that day.

I decided to insert my maturity since I was now attending class at the young-adult level. I told the girls that I was going back upstairs to my class and that they should do the same and that I would see them at the eleven o'clock service.

As I was walking up the stairs back to the main sanctuary, the telephone in the clerks' office was ringing. The office was parallel to the stairway separated by a long hallway. I saw Mr. Wilson, the superintendent of Adult Sunday School, rushing toward the clerks' office. He frantically told me to get back to my class and said that he would answer the phone. I was a little surprised by his tone because he always had a calm demeanor. Before I got comfortable in my seat, a loud sound like thunder roared through the church. My sister and I looked at each other with awe because there were no clouds in the sky on our way to church that indicated rain. And the weather forecast did not indicate rain for that day. Mr. Wilson, who had just spoken to me in an unusual tone, ran into the sanctuary and told us to evacuate the building as fast as we could because the church was being bombed. Those of us in the main sanctuary were in disbelief until the building started shaking fiercely and the stained-glass windows began to crumble. Glass flew through the sanctuary like bullets. It felt like the building was going to collapse. I remember Ann grabbing my hand as we crawled toward the front door of the church. Once we managed to get down the steps to the ground, we were both shaking and grasping to catch our breath. Then I screamed, "Oh my God, Karen is in the basement." When we saw the frightened children scrambling to get out of the basement, some of the children and adults were covered with dusty debris, we spotted Karen in the crowd with the other children. We were so glad that she got out unharmed, because her parents trusted us to take care of their daughter until they arrived for the eleven o'clock service. The adults who were in the main sanctuary that had children in the basement of the church were screaming their children's names. We were so shaken that we didn't know what to do. We were all standing around in a daze. From the front of the church, it appeared that everything was all right and everyone got out without any serious injuries. But it turned out that some of the children were injured, and some were missing. One of the parents screamed, "My God they bombed our children!"

The Birmingham Police Department had already surrounded and blocked the area around the church by the time everyone was able to get out of the church. The police and firemen arrived so quickly that it appeared as if they already knew ahead of time when the explosion was going to happen. The explosion was so loud that it was heard throughout the city. When the stunning news raced through the Black community, crowds of people young and old from the surrounding neighborhood gathered around the church to help those who were injured. The pastor, John Cross, urged everyone to try and remain calm. He also urged those who had not sustained injuries to go home. The other church leaders tried to keep everyone away from the Sixteenth Street side of the church where the bomb exploded. The explosion blew a massive hole through the lady's lounge area in the basement of the church. The concrete steps on the Sixteenth Street side of the church that led up to the main level to the pastor's office were chunks of demolished mortar thrown about the street. The small rectangular window in the ladies' lounge located behind the steps was where the bomb had apparently been placed. That was the location where the ticking sound came from that I heard when I was in the lounge before the explosion. The explosion shattered windows in the buildings across the street and demolished several cars that were parked near the church. All the stained-glass windows in the main sanctuary were shattered except one window-pane with a picture of Jesus walking with a child remained mostly intact. Only the face of Jesus was damaged by the blast.

As the medical personnel arrived and began to care for the injured, the crowd of onlookers grew larger. Some of the people were assisting the rescue workers to dig through the rubble searching for the missing children. When I heard that the first missing child pulled from the rubble was decapitated, I became weak in the knees and almost fainted. Later, I heard that the other children were found almost within the same location and their bodies were horribly mangled. However, another child badly injured who was dug from under large slabs of concrete and stones was screaming for her sister, who was one of the victims who did not survive. At that time, I did not know the names of the victims. Knowing in my heart that the girls who were in the lounge with me earlier had gone back to their Sunday school classes could not be the victims.

The news that our mothers received was that the church had been completely demolished and that there were no survivors. That same news was received by my dad in Washington, DC. Before our mother and Karen's mother and father reached the Sixteenth Street area, Karen's grandmother who was not a member of the church arrived on the scene and took my sister, Karen, and me home. So when our parents arrived on the scene, I am sure they were in a frantic state of mind. After seeing that the church was not completely demolished, I know they must have felt somewhat relieved and panic set in when they could not find us. They probably thought we were the victims of the bombings. One of our church members informed them that we had not been injured and that Karen's grandmother Ludie Bailey took us home. Mrs. Bailey had arrived early for the eleven o'clock service. She often visited the church on special occasions when Karen and her grandson Ronald were playing special roles in the church service.

After our mother and Karen's parents arrived back on the west side of town, Mother tried to call our dad to let him know that we were safe and had not been injured in the explosion but was able to make the connection. My mother was surprised and shocked when I fainted after she told me the names of the children who did not survive. After Mother managed to revive me and found out that I had talked to the girls just before the explosion, she fully understood my reactions to the news. The only words I could utter were, "It could have been me… Oh my God, it could have been me." I kept screaming. I could not believe what I had heard, because I thought the girls had gone back to their classes. If I had stayed and continued to socialize with my friends, I would have been a victim too. God's grace spared my life. But in my mind, I wondered why my friends did not receive that favor and mercy. How will I ever be able to forget our last conversation before I made my way back up to the main sanctuary? I know God loved them as much as he loves me. I imagine the divine plan for my life was not supposed to end at that moment when the bomb exploded. I had no idea about the complete picture of God's plan for my life as a survivor. My mind was in a state of confusion. I could not feel happiness or prosperity. Life appeared dismal and dark. All I could do was try to stay alert and trust God's will for my life. I have been led to believe that our Creator had a reason for allowing things to happen as they happened. However, I will never understand or know his wisdom, but I trusted his will for my future. At the same time, doubt was trying to cloud my mind because my friends did not survive. Being a young Christian, I had to learn how to take a stand on my faith and believe that the horrible event happened to give me an opportunity to demonstrate my perseverance and measure my spiritual maturity. I needed to trust and believe that grace and the power of the Spirit would help me move forward and overcome that unforgettable day that shamed the nation. In my heart, I had to believe that, no matter what, I would be okay.

Chapter 3

If we live, it's to honor the Lord. And if we die, it's to honor the Lord. So whether we live or die, we belong to the Lord.

—Romans 14:8

I was having a hard time believing that my Sunday school friends were victims of cruel madness, vile bigotry, and deadly hatred by unknown persons. The Black community was stunned to a point of disbelief for justice to prevail. The whole world had been affected by their deaths. There are no words to say, and nothing could be done that would undo or make up for their deaths. The evil-hearted individual or individuals who interrupted the worship service with such a heinous crime should be ashamed for carrying out such a disgraceful disruption at the house of worship. Maybe the conscience of the individual or individuals who carried out that disgraceful act of terror does not exist. It was a cowardly act by a demented fool or fools that will never be forgotten. Even today, the bombing of the church is an act of terror that's on the list with the other terroristic events that occurred after that shameful day.

The last words I had with the girls will resonate in my mind and heart forever. Carol and I both attended Parker High School. We were also members of the same Girl Scout Troop at the church and attended the same dance school on Saturday afternoons at the Smithfield Recreation Center to get lessons in tap, ballet, and modern dances. Cynthia attended Ullman High School, which is now part of the University of Alabama Birmingham (UAB). Cynthia was also a member of the Girl Scout Troop with Carol and me at the church. Cynthia had a quiet and sweet spirit. She was an only child, who was adored by her parents. The Westleys adopted Cynthia when she was very young. My mother and the Westleys were close friends outside of the church relationship. Denise, several years younger, was an only child with a sweet, loving, and kind spirit. She exuded a spirit of love and happiness all the time. Denise was loved dearly by her parents and grandparents. Denise's father, Chris McNair, was my vocational education teacher at Parker High School. Mr. McNair was also an accomplished photographer and former state legislator, now deceased. I learned photography and film development through his leadership. Addie Mae, a year younger than me, was a church friend. She was a quiet, sweet girl from a large loving family. Her oldest sister, Junie, a year older than me, was in the same Sunday school class with me and my sister and attended Parker High School as well. Addie and her sisters rarely missed attending Sunday school and church. Although we all came from different family dynamics, we were all learning how to live our lives to shine the light of Christ.

Once the reality of the fact that the church had been bombed and there were actually victims from the heinous crime, life would never be the same for me, the families of the victims, and their friends who loved them. I knew that I would never be able to forget the images of their faces and our last conversation before the explosion. I also had to embrace my pain and sorrow about the heinous crime. My heart was broken into pieces that could not be made whole again. But I took comfort in knowing that God would punish the evil people. Although there had been dozens of unsolved bombings that had terrorized the Black communities where the civil rights leaders lived for more than a decade, in this case, innocent lives were taken. This heinous crime was the first difficult challenge I had ever faced in my life. The thought often pondered, What is so bad or wrong with Black people that some White people felt that we should be punished by death for no valid or justifiable reason other than the color of our skin and that we did not deserve the right to be here on earth? I also wondered why some White Americans were so fearful of our presence when the facts of history remind me that White Americans, as immigrants, came to America for a better life and brought my ancestors against their will to America to help build this nation, yet they were determined not to allow us to share in the prosperity of this nation.

The victory on behalf of school integration apparently was not well received by the violent racist group, the Ku Klux Klan. Birmingham was the haven for the most violent Ku Klux Klan chapter in the South. Bombings and killings by police had terrorized the Black community since World War II. The Sixteenth Street Baptist Church bombing was the fourth bombing within four weeks that occurred in the city of Birmingham after the school desegregation crisis came to a boil on September 4, 1963. With so many unsolved racial bombings in the city, Birmingham acquired the nickname "Bombingham."

After the bombing of the church and the death of the four girls, the tension in the air clouded the city with fear, sorrow, and shame. There was a feeling of diminishing faith in city hall to measure up to the responsibility of the kind of municipal leadership needed to manage and keep the people in the city safe. The mayor of the city, Albert Boutwell expressed his concerns regarding the bombing. He said, "It was a tragic and sickening event to know that a few individuals could commit such a horrible atrocity." Dr. King wired Governor Wallace and told him that "The blood of four little children was on his hands, and his irresponsible and misguided actions created in the city of Birmingham and the state of Alabama an atmosphere that induced continued violence and now murder." A week before the bombing, Governor Wallace told the *New York Times* that to stop school integration, that Alabama needed a "few first-class funerals."

The church bombing triggered outbreaks of violence all over the city that left two other Black youth dead. Several Black-owned businesses were destroyed by fire, but there were no major injuries. The city council held an emergency meeting to discuss safety measures for the city but decided against placing a curfew on the city. The NAACP executive secretary, Roy Wilkins, wired President Kennedy to get assistance from the federal government before the Black communities employ whatever methods necessary in defense of the lives of the Black people in Birmingham. President Kennedy ordered his chief civil rights troubleshooter, Burk Marshall, to go to

Birmingham, along with FBI agents who were bomb experts. Martin Luther King Jr. wired President Kennedy from Atlanta to inform him that he was going to Birmingham to plead with the Black communities to remain nonviolent. However, he said that unless "immediate federal steps are taken, there will be in Birmingham and the state of Alabama the worst racial holocaust this nation has ever seen." From that request by Dr. King, reinforced police units patrolled the city, and Governor Wallace ordered National Guardsmen to stand by at a Birmingham armory.

Meanwhile, on the west side of Birmingham in my community, I felt a little safer from the violence that erupted on the north side since our house was on a dead-end street where no major events took place. Our little dead-end street, to me, seemed isolated and disconnected from the rest of the community. However, knowing the fact that the Klan could strike anywhere, the atmosphere in Black communities was filled with unquenchable fear and anger. The fear stemmed from all the unsolved bombings prior to the church bombing and the fear of the police and their lack of sincerity of public safety and security for all the citizens of the city of Birmingham. The Black communities were angry regarding the insanity, intolerance, disrespect of the House of Worship, defiance of established laws, and disregard of Black Americans' human values. All the unsolved racial bombings suggested that the fabric of the society in the city of Birmingham had deteriorated. The city known as "Bombingham" was sick from fear, sorrow, and shame. The House of Worship was at war with society. The integrity and power of the church were in jeopardy. I could not comprehend how some members of our society thought that the murder of innocent children in the House of Worship was an act of justice and revenge against the integration of the public schools. When the House of Worship and the schoolhouse are in jeopardy, society has no hope or respect for human worth and values. I believe, and I am sure other believers feel, that the House of Worship is a sacred place to assemble together its members to bring them to spiritual maturity (Ephesians 4:13) and reach out to spread the love of Christ and the gospel message to unbelievers in the world (Matthew 28:18–20). Clearly, the person or persons who committed the heinous and cowardly crime of bombing the church definitely could not be believers in Christ.

American educational philosophers such as John Dewey, George Counts, and Mortimer Adler all agreed that American schools serve a wide variety of purposes. They all agreed that the primary role of schooling is to equip individuals to live as productive members of our society. Somewhere in the minds and hearts of the bomber or bombers, this idea was lost or forgotten. Or perhaps, to them, Black Americans have no place in society. To me, it appeared that the rights and opportunities for Black Americans in our society were at stake. The laws did not appear to respect our values and worth. Yet God's Word instructs me, as a believer, not to worry about the wicked or envy those who do wrong, because they are like grass and spring flowers that soon fade and wither away (Psalm 37:1–2).

I'm thinking at this point, the efforts to end racial discrimination in Birmingham, Alabama, and change the hearts and minds of some White Americans were at risk. The city needed a cultural transformation that would promote the kind of society that respected the values of all its citizens. The possibility of a cultural transformation seemed uncertain. But I had to continue to believe that the power to change the uncertainty was in the hands of our *divine Creator*. I believe that is why the heinous and cowardly crime committed by the evil individual or individuals did not cause much more devastation. In spite of the loss of innocent lives, as a believer, I had to continue to trust in the Lord and do good so that I could continue to live safely and receive what my heart desires (Psalm 37:3–4), freedom, equality, and justice.

When night fell on the city of Birmingham after the bombing, every sound I heard was like the sound of glass breaking or loud thunder. I was too afraid to close my eyes. When I did, I would see the stained-glass windows crumbling and feel the vibration of the building shaking. Watching television made matters worse because the bombing event was all the news reporters talked about, along with all the other craziness that was happening in the city. Just about the time when my sister and I were preparing for bed, the doorbell rang. We were all frightened because that was unusual at our house for anyone to ring the doorbell at that hour of the night. My sister and I went to the door with Mother. When Mother turned on the porch light and saw our dad, she said that she almost wet herself in shock. Mother had been trying to reach my dad to let him know that we were safe, but all efforts had failed. We were so happy to see him. He told us that he was expecting the worst because of the news he received in Washington, DC, that the church was completely demolished and scores of people were hurt and dead. He went on to tell us how hard it was to get a flight to Birmingham at a minute's notice. He had to fly standby, and his layover time in Atlanta was three hours long. Dad said he tried calling once he got to Atlanta, but the telephone line kept giving a busy signal.

This was the first time my dad came home with no luggage. All he had was on his back. I imagine he was a shaken man when he left Washington, DC, not knowing if he would find his family dead or alive, because he knew we always went to church. With all the excitement, our baby brother, Edmond, woke up. When he saw our dad, he jumped with joy because it had only been fifteen days since we returned to Birmingham from Washington, DC, from our summer vacation. I felt a sense of calmness with my dad being there to protect the family. Even though I knew Dad would only be in Birmingham for a short time, I found the strength to believe that God could make something beautiful out of a difficult situation. In my mind, I was wishing we could leave Birmingham forever and go live in Washington, DC, all together as a family. Even though my sister and I only played a small part in the Civil Rights Movement during the children's crusade protest, deep inside, I felt vulnerable to the way life was unraveling before my eyes in Birmingham. The uncertainty of the future for Black Americans, especially in the city of Birmingham, was a heavy burden for any teenage girl or boy to have to bear.

The days leading up to the funeral for the four girls were very difficult. It was hard to focus on the fact that I was blessed and my life had been spared. All I could think about was the moments before the bomb exploded. The image of the smiles on their faces and the joy and excitement about the upcoming youth day service will never be forgotten. That youth day service was stolen from us. We were robbed of the opportunity to worship and glorify our Lord and Savior that day. Cynthia, Addie, Carol, and Denise were robbed of their opportunity to become adults and explore their dreams and aspirations. Their families were robbed of the opportunity to see them become adults and explore all that the world had to offer.

The funeral service for Carol Roberson was held at St. John AME Church on September 17, 1963. Her family requested a private ceremony with close family and friends. On September 18, 1963, the combined funeral service for the other three girls was held at Sixth Avenue Baptist Church, the second-largest Black American congregation in Birmingham at that time. Inside the church sanctuary, hundreds of mourners gathered to pay their last tribute of respect to God's beautiful children. Outside, under a hot September sun, hundreds of more mourners stood along the streets to pay their final respects to the innocent and beautiful children. All the civil rights leaders were there. Dr. Martin Luther King Jr. gave the eulogy for the three young girls. Dr. King spoke to the hearts and minds of the audience. He told the audience that even though the girls were the victims of one of the most vicious and tragic crimes ever perpetrated against humanity, they died nobly and they are the martyred heroines of a holy crusade for freedom and human dignity. They did not die in vain. God has a way of bringing good out of evil. The innocent blood of the little girls may well serve as a redemptive force that will bring new light to the dark city of Birmingham and lead the whole Southland from the low road of man's inhumanity to man's high road of peace and brotherhood. The spilled blood of the innocent girls may cause the whole citizenry of Birmingham to transform the negative extremes of a dark past into the positive extremes of a bright future and cause the White South to come to terms with its conscience.

As I sat and listened to the words spoken by Dr. King, my mind kept wandering back to the Sunday morning when the bomb exploded. It was hard to hear the words "We must not despair, we must not become bitter, nor must we harbor the desire to retaliate with violence, and we must not lose faith in our White brothers." In some way, we must believe that the most misguided among them can learn to respect the dignity and the worth of all human personalities. As Dr. King was speaking words of encouragement to the families of the victims, I thought, *What if it happens again right here and now while we are paying our last tribute of respect to the innocent children who were already gone?* Then I heard Dr. King say that death will come to every individual because death is not an aristocracy for some of the people but a democracy for all the people. Death is the irreducible common denominator for all humans. But from Christianity's affirmation, death is not the end. Death is not a period that ends the great sentence of life but a comma that punctuates it to more lofty significance. Death is not a blind alley that leads the human race into a state of nothingness but an open door which leads us into eternal life.

As I listened to the conclusion of Dr. King's message, I was trying to find some consolation from my faith to lift myself from despair to hope so that I could believe that the death of my four friends would symbolize a new day especially since they died between the sacred walls of the House of Worship. At that point, I could not visualize the future for the city of Birmingham. Through my eyes, Birmingham needed healing from the curse of racial hatred and injustice toward Black Americans. The city needed compassion, mercy, and hope—the hope that would fulfill Dr. King's promise that everyone is judged not by the color of their skin but by the content of their character. The hope that the leaders of the city of Birmingham would uphold the Constitution—despite being marred by the original sin of slavery—regarding the idea of equal citizenship under the law for all Americans.

My hometown would never be the same. The individuals responsible for killing the innocent girls challenged the conscience of decent people everywhere. Decent people with a righteous heart and conscience could not stand on the sideline in the struggle for justice against the evil system of segregation. The system must be transformed. The way of life and the philosophy that produced individuals who could murder innocent people needed to end. Dr. King said,

"We must work passionately and unrelentingly for the realization of the American dream." The idea of the American dream is rooted back in the founding fathers in their formulation of the Constitution and the Declaration of Independence. The meaning of the American dream has changed throughout history. But the ethos then and today implies an opportunity for life to be better, richer, and fuller for everyone, with an opportunity for each individual according to their ability or achievement. The dream of social order in which every individual shall be able to attain the fullest stature of which they are innately capable and be recognized by others for who they are, regardless of the fortuitous circumstances of birth or position.

In my mind and heart, it felt like the American dream died. The dream for social order seemed uncertain. But I had to keep hope alive and trust that God would work to make the death of the innocent girls something beautiful. I could not imagine the pain and grief the families of the innocent girls felt. But the pain I felt as their friend was unquenchable. When the three coffins holding the remains of my friends rolled out of the sanctuary to go to their final resting place, my heart dropped to my feet. I could not move from where I was standing without the aid of my mother's arms around me. I could not comprehend my feeling of threat and fear. I tried to focus on Psalm 23:4: I will fear no evil, for thou art with me… I was trying to remove the fear of harm from my mind because God's words told me that his rod and staff would comfort me and that he would prepare a table before me in the presence of my enemies. But at the same time, the heinous crime and cowardly act of bombing the House of Worship that caused the death of my friends did actually happen. I was afraid to face the darkness of what was before me; and I was having trouble surrendering my desire to be in control because the world, as I could see, during that time was filled with so many obstacles that thrived on fear. I was fearful that I had no chance for the future. But at the same time, a voice inside told me not to give in to my fears and not allow fear to control my life. Somewhere in my mind and heart, I had to find some hope so that I would not be consumed with fear. I had to be strong, courageous, and confident in spite of the horrible experience and look fear in the face. I survived a horrible event. And I needed to be strong to take on the next challenge that would come my way.

Days after the church bombing, the nation's outcry for justice was enormous. Law enforcement agents vowed to leave no stones unturned until the perpetrators of the heinous crime were brought to justice. The Alabama State troopers and the Birmingham City police joined forces in an all-out effort to identify and apprehend the killers of the four innocent girls. A reward fund was established to get individuals to come forward with information that would help with the identity of the perpetrators. At that time, the Ku Klux Klan members were under scrutiny. Some of the Klan members became paid informers for the FBI. Three Birmingham men—Charles Cage, John Wesley Hall, and Robert Chambliss—were arrested on charges of possessing dynamite. The three men had been observed near the church on the day of the explosion. However, the charges against the three men were overturned even though investigators believed they were involved in the bombing. Robert Chambliss, who was called "Dynamite Bob," was well-known in Birmingham as an outspoken racist and a suspect in previous bombings. Chambliss was also a known member of the Ku Klux Klan who had a favorable relationship with the Birmingham City Police Department that made him untouchable. In the meantime, the outcome of the suspended charges against the three men gave the Klan more fuel to spread their twisted vision of America. It was reported in the news that at a hate rally in Florida, the Klan leader said the death of the four girls means that there are "four less 'niggers' today" and praised the individuals who planted the bomb as having done a good thing.

The Klan's vision of the American dream certainly did not include Black Americans. But no American with a conscience could brush aside the magnitude of the evil crime done by this group of individuals. The best that I could do as a young teenage girl was to remind myself that the voice of reason or the force of compromise would create a society of liberty and justice for all citizens. I was left to believe that we must continue to carry on the fight for civil and human rights and believe in the divine goodness of God to strengthen us through challenging times.

The day-to-day struggles to survive under the Jim Crow laws were truly challenging times. Even though the protest march for freedom and justice ended in May 1963 with the agreement from the leaders of the city of Birmingham to make changes that would include Black Americans as legal citizens and open doors to opportunities within the city, there were still barriers preventing that from happening. The visible signs of discrimination were removed from the water fountains, the restrooms, the lunch counters, and public transportation; but as humans, we were still segregated. Governor Wallace had vowed that the state of Alabama would be segregated now and forever. Governor Wallace had a deadly tongue and evil motives toward Black Americans. In spite of his vow, by the end of September 1963, a few Black children were attending a few of the predominantly White schools. But the majority of Blacks were attending the predominantly Black schools, and the majority of Whites were attending the predominantly White schools. The cloud of fear and distrust lingering between Blacks and Whites in the city left little to no room for healing and bringing the city together. The cloud of fear that White Americans faced was how to maintain power and control of the city. The city needed divine intervention to drive away from the darkness. Through my eyes, I could not see any light, but I held onto hope.

The bomb caused substantial damage to the basement area of the church and the interior of the main sanctuary. But the main structure of the building stood strong. The damages, however, were substantial enough that worship services could not be held at the church. From the end of September 1963 to the first Sunday in June 1964, worship service was held at the A. G. Gaston auditorium, a facility that was part of the Booker T. Washington Business College owned by the wealthiest Black businessman in Birmingham, A. G. Gaston. It was not the typical setting of a church sanctuary; but where there are two or three who gather in the name of the Lord, his Spirit is in the midst.

When worship services first started at the auditorium, the attendance was not the same as before the bombing for whatever reasons. But as time went on, attendance began to increase. I have to admit, I was reluctant at first to attend because I thought the bomber or bombers would strike again since this location was only a block from the church's location. I am sure it is safe to say that most of the members felt some reluctance. But all things work together for the good of those who love God and are called together for his purpose (Romans 8:28), and then no one can be against us. We were like the Israelites when they reached the Jordan River. We were standing on the edge. As members of the body of Christ, we had to engage in a test of faith. By exercising faith, the congregation was able to see that the power of God was with us and allowed us to move forward until the restoration of the church was completed.

While the eyes of the world were still watching Birmingham, there was some calmness in the atmosphere. However, the cloud of fear still lingered in the air. Although FBI agents were already in position to investigate the previous series of bombings and followed up on hundreds of leads related to the church bombing, the Black leaders and the Black communities within the city were not satisfied with the outcome of the investigations. Months passed and no arrests were made for the church bombing. In addition to the three suspects—Cage, Hall, and Chambliss—the FBI had suspicions about three other individuals: Bobby Frank Cherry, Herman Frank Cash, and Thomas Blanton Jr., all members of a local Klan group called the Eastview 13 Klavern. The day-to-day struggle for civil rights and justice for Black Americans continued to hang on the unbalanced scale of justice. The director of the FBI, J. Edgar Hoover, at that time did not approve the arrest of the individuals because he felt that prosecutors would not be able to get a conviction in any court in the South. That was a prime example of two justice systems. Hoover believed that the Black Civil Rights Movement was under the control of foreign and domestic communists. He also referenced Martin

Luther King Jr. as a communist and a troublemaker. It was clear that Hoover was allowing wrong to triumphed instead of doing his job to solve the bombing cases. All the information collected by the FBI agents about the bombing was never passed on to the Department of Justice. The wicked seems to go unpunished while the righteous suffer. For the sake of maintaining a sound mind, maintaining an unhardened heart, and not being angry, I had to believe that justice would ultimately prevail and the wicked individuals would pay for their crimes. At the same time, I could not allow anger and rage to consume my thoughts. Life is so brief!

It was not easy going about day by day and not being reminded of the injustice. I had to find a way to live in acceptance and keep my faith strong while I wait for the outcome of justice for all involved. I was at a point in my life where I needed to tune in and focus on choosing the right path and making the right decisions for my life. But I couldn't see the right path for me while living in Birmingham. My parents always tried to shield me and my sister from the ugly truth of racism. However, I was wise enough to see what was real. While at home, school, and church, and in my neighborhood, the only people I encountered were people who looked like me. As I mentioned earlier, my community at the time was surrounded by a White community of White people who were invisible to me, and I am sure the Black people in my community were invisible to the White people, and we were just a stone's throw away from each other. Yet outside the safety net of my community, there was a society of White Americans who wished Black Americans didn't exist. Even after the visible signs of segregation were removed from public places, most of the powerful and privileged were still not open-minded toward allowing Black Americans the opportunity to have a share of what the world had to offer.

Reflecting back to 1941, before I was born, when Franklin D. Roosevelt gave his State of the Union address, he spoke about four essential freedoms that the world was founded upon: freedom of speech, freedom of worship, freedom from want, and freedom from fear. All of these freedoms are essential for all humans.

Through my eyes, Black Americans in Birmingham and other parts of the Southland, freedom from fear was at the forefront. And freedom from want was trailing close behind. Every American desires to have the ability to live life without having to endure violence and hatred. But Black Americans in Birmingham and other parts of the Southland were being denied the option to have freedom from fear by a small group of selfish individuals. Those selfish individuals kept the cloud of fear lingering in the atmosphere. As long as the individuals who took the lives of the four innocent girls go unpunished for their crime of murder, the cloud of fear would continue to linger in the atmosphere. Fear is a natural response to the challenges that we face in life, but at the same time, fear tells us to be cautious and stay alert and be prepared to face what comes our way. I knew that I had to find a way to confront my freedom from fear. I survived the church bombing for a purpose, and there should be no reason for me to fear mere mortals.

Even though I was clear about what I wanted in life, I was allowing things beyond my control to clutter my mind to the point that I couldn't hear myself think. I knew that I needed to focus on finishing high school so that I could make my exit from the city of fear, sorrow, and shame, so that I could also experience the freedom from want that FDR spoke about in his State of the Union address. I was looking forward to a healthy and peaceful nation with a shared economic system for all of its inhabitants. Although FDR spoke about civil liberties for all and a healthy peacetime life for all its inhabitants in 1941, clearly through my eyes in 1963, this was not the case for Black Americans in Birmingham and other parts of the Southland. I felt like I was in a tunnel of discouragement that was trying to sap energy and joy from my life. But despite the multiple sources of opposition I faced, somehow, I found the courage and confidence to keep walking toward the light, the light of hope and promise. And the balance of justice was just ahead to snuff out the power of the wicked and evil individuals. So that the sparks of evil fire would not continue to grow. At the proper time, justice would prevail.

Part 2

Reclaiming My Hope

Chapter 4

Having hope will give you courage.

—Job 11:18

When I was much younger, I had a hard time comprehending Jesus's teaching about loving our enemies and praying for those who persecute you (Matthew 5:43–44)! For me, that was a radical response to injustice. All the hatred and violence that most Southern White Americans invoked on Black Americans during the Jim Crow era and the Civil Rights Movement era made that teaching of love almost incomprehensible. How do you give justice and mercy to the ones who oppress you? My faith in hope for justice was challenged. My hope had been uprooted like a fallen tree. When I reflected on the story about Job and how he was able to overcome, I somewhat felt that I could believe that there could be hope for justice. A question lingered in my mind: *How could any human disrespect the House of Worship and take the lives of innocent children?* The only answer to the question that I could come up with is sin. Sin is the root of all evil and wrongdoing. Sin causes you to do wrong and think it is right. The individuals who carried out the heinous crime of bombing the House of Worship committed an offense against religious and moral laws. Their act of evil was so flagrant it could not be ignored, hidden under the rug, and just forgotten. As I mentioned earlier, the FBI investigation had identified the known Klan members as suspects in the church bombing. But the investigation was closed, and no charges were filed against the extremely wicked and evil individuals. The actions by the FBI gave me more reasons to believe that hope for justice for Black Americans was dead. Holding onto faith and hope that the individuals who interrupted the worship service would be punished was very difficult under the current justice system. It appeared that justice was being denied to the righteous and twisted in favor of the wicked. Somehow and someway, true justice had to prevail for the four girls and their families, and the rest of us who experienced that atrocity firsthand!

The tragedy regarding the church bombing challenged the core of my soul. Aside from school, going to church was the center of my life. All of us who were at the church when the bomb exploded could have been victims. Which raised other questions that lingered in my mind: *Why did I survive? Was it the power of faith that ordered my steps? Was it a divine plan? Why did God's grace and mercy deliver me and the other survivors from harm?* The simple answer to my first question had to be grace and mercy through faith that I survived along with the other survivors. Then I had to ask, why didn't Cynthia, Denise, Addie, and Carol deserve to receive that same grace and mercy? The answer to that question was beyond my understanding. But what I realize now is that having faith is essential to living in this physical world and believing that faith is the substance that keeps doubt from consuming my hopes.

Knowing that life's journey consists of a set of divine boundaries that govern the past, present, and future, I had hopes that divine justice would intervene. When I think back to the time when Noah received instructions to build the ark before the flood and Noah followed through, only Noah and his family and the creatures on the boat with Noah survived. When I was in the ladies' lounge with the girls, no one heard the ticking sound coming from the location by the window but me. They all looked at me as if something was wrong with me when I asked if they heard what I was hearing. Since no one else heard the ticking, I even thought that maybe I was just hearing things. Was that a sign meant for only me to hear? The steps that I took to go to the basement of the church to get to the ladies' lounge could have been my last steps. But I was given unmerited divine assistance to get back upstairs to the main sanctuary before the bomb exploded. Did I survive because the voice inside told me to get back upstairs? I had no idea that would be the last time I would see my friends. But an act of evil injustice interrupted the Youth Day plans. I know, as humans, we cannot see the whole scope of our life's plans from the beginning to the end. There was no reason for me to think that I would not see my friends again as I made my way back up the stairs. After the teaching of the Sunday school lesson, all the classes would assemble together to hear the highlights of the lesson and hear the financial report from each class before the break and the beginning of the eleven o'clock service when everyone gathered together in the main sanctuary. But that did not happen that Sunday.

Based on my Christian belief and understanding, a divine plan comes directly from God and is supremely good. This means that the church bombing was definitely not a divine plan or the will of God. For that reason, alone, my hope for justice for the evil act of injustice must prevail. My hope was that the will of God would avenge the blood of his children and judgment for the evil individuals who bombed the church would come soon. The four girls and their families needed justice. True justice needed to prevail. The bombers acted corruptly and perversely against the will of God. Their hearts must have been filled with deceit and hate to carry out such an evil act.

The world around me and people like me had been invoked with hatred and discrimination for as long as I can remember. Growing up under such inhumane conditions made life seem unfair. I kept hoping that life in Birmingham could be a better place for all the people since we are all children of the same Creator. Segregation and discrimination were concepts and beliefs created by some White people to distort the truth. The notion that some people were inherently better than others because of skin color is wrong and unjustified. We were all made in the image and likeness of God, capable of expressing miraculous wholeness, abundance, and well-being. The idea that a group of selfish individuals (the Ku Klux Klan) manifested as a hate group to invoke violence against Black Americans to try to purify American society was downright evil and vicious. The first movement of the KKK's or the Klan flourished in the Southern United States in the late 1860s and disbanded by the early 1870s. The second Klan movement flourished nationwide in the early and mid-1920s and adopted a standard White costume with masks and conical hats to hide their identities. They terrified the nation with burning crosses, lynching, and mass parades. The third Klan movement emerged after 1950 in opposition to the Civil Rights Movement because of the progress being made by Black Americans. They reign unforgettable acts of terror on the Southland. The Klan members saw themselves as holding to White American values and Christian morality. Black Americans did not fit the dominant American culture: White Anglo-Saxon Protestant male mold or shape. Black Americans are identifiably different, so the exclusion of Black Americans from the dominant culture was the right idea that some White Americans (Klan members) felt was right and just. Holding to Christian morality meant that they believed that the best way to live is in keeping with the teaching of Jesus, including loving God and your neighbors, living by the Ten Commandments and the Golden Rule. Clearly, the Klan members did not apply God's laws given their destructive public behavior.

I have been led to believe that most Americans practice Christianity or some form of faith. But during the 1960s, it was hard to believe that fact because of the reign of terror that had been invoked on the Black communities and the Black churches. People who profess to be Christians and believe in God are led by the Spirit to do what is right and good and to love your neighbor. Hatred and discrimination are not right and definitely not good. Destroying the House of Worship was not right and definitely not good. If faith and hope had power, then its ability should be challenged to correct the wrong of bombing the church and taking the lives of the four innocent girls. According to the scripture, "The Lord is slow to get angry, but his power is great, and he never lets the guilty go unpunished" (Nahum 1:3). I believed with my whole heart that God was angry and disappointed about the actions of the bombers on September 15, 1963, at 10:22 a.m. and that he would take revenge on the evil individuals and at the same time provide refuge for the families of the innocent girls and the rest of us who survived the bombing. I believed God and no one else could provide both justice and mercy.

As I mentioned earlier, I have struggled with several questions that led to more questions than answers. So the question "*Why did God's grace and mercy deliver me and the other survivors from harm?*" has been a tremendous challenge to my mind. Which moved me in a direction to rely on faith as my system of support to help sustain me through the worst challenges that I have encountered in life. But I could not imagine or think of an answer to the question. Perhaps it was grace and mercy that shielded and sustained us—that same grace and mercy that shielded and protected the protesters from the pain inflicted upon them by the high pressure of the water from the fire hoses and the vicious dogs. It was also their faith that put them on the front line of harm and danger. However, I couldn't imagine why my four innocent friends did not receive the grace and mercy that delivered me and the other survivors from harm when the bomb exploded. I thought God's grace and mercy are for everyone. They were branches that were severed from the vine not because they were not producing fruit. They were severed from the vine by evil individuals who were already cut off at the trunk because the evil individuals were trying to block the efforts of God's will.

There had to be some purpose behind the immeasurable loss. Jesus's death on the Cross was a day of confusion and uncertainty, but all was not lost on that day. For those of us who believe in the inerrancy of the Bible, we have to remember the promises in the Bible and the words of Jesus that a new day was coming. I am sure the parents of the innocent girls wanted an answer to the tragic loss of their daughters. Was there an answer that would right the wrong? The parents of the innocent girls needed retributive justice, not vengeance. Retribution is directed only at the wrongs; it is not personal and does not involve pleasure at the suffering of others, but the murderers needed to be punished for the wrong they had done. The idea of that immeasurable loss to happen to let justice roll down like water and righteousness flow like a mighty stream was beyond my comprehension at age fifteen. I was struggling to understand and deal with the concept of justice as it related to Black Americans. According to research, the concept of justice includes both the attainment of that which is just and the philosophical discussion of that which is just.

As a Black American, my thought was, How do we attain that which is just aside from the philosophical discussion of that which is just? The concept of justice is based on numerous fields and many differing viewpoints and perspectives. The concept of moral correctness based on law, ethics, religion, and fairness was my main concern as it relates to what is just. Since the philosophical discussion of justice is divided into the realm of social justice as found in philosophy, theology, and religion, and procedural justice as found in the study and application of the law, then the murderers of the innocent girls should receive the punishment that fits the crime. In Deuteronomy 19:17–21 and Exodus 21:23, justice includes the punishment of life for a life… That attitude toward punishment is primitive, but it was actually a breakthrough for justice and fairness in ancient times. The principle of making the punishment fit the crime should still be observed today. Yet the justice department was unable to bring the murderers to trial for the heinous crime of bombing the church. The fight to win the battle over evil and injustice still hung in the balance of injustice and burned in the hearts and minds of Black Americans as unjust. Black Americans needed a breakthrough for justice. The Black community needed fair retribution for the wrong that had been done. Not just for the bombing of the church and the death of the four innocent girls but for more than a hundred years of inhumane treatment and an unequal world of disenfranchisement, oppression, and racial violence.

Over the years, Black Americans were forced to adapt to the mainstream values and behaviors of the dominant American culture; and at the same time because of our identifiable difference, we were rejected and excluded from the dominant culture. But in spite of rejection and exclusion, we were not crushed and driven to despair. There had to be a divine plan. That is not to say that the senseless death of the four innocent girls was a divine plan, or was it? As I mentioned earlier, Governor George Wallace told a reporter from the *New York Times* that Alabama needed "a few first-class funerals." He made that comment a week before the church was bombed about school integration. Based on that comment, one would be led to believe that the church bombing was a plan but not a *divine* plan.

What good could come from this wrong? Nothing could be said or done to make up for that immeasurable loss. Even though the parents of the four innocent girls received consoling words and comfort from knowing that their children were gone to a better place, my thought was, they went to that place way too soon. I have to carry that thought in my head forever and yet be able to continue to live my life with hope and aspirations that I would be able to achieve the American dream—the dream that assures everyone is equal in status or at least ought to be given an equal opportunity to achieve status through hard work. But the justice system through my eyes at age fifteen was not working for the benefit of Black Americans. I refused to let fear make me afraid that things were not going to get better. I have to admit that as time went on and it seemed that no progress was being made for justice to prevail, I had to remind myself that when things work per divine law, miracles will manifest, and the death of my four friends would not be in vain.

As I approached the age of understanding, I often asked my parents why White people did not like Black people. They could never answer that question with any words that made sense to me. Maybe because we had family members who looked like White people. When my dad took us to visit his family in Livingston, Alabama, during the Christmas holiday, I remember thinking, *Why was this man who looked White always in my grandmother's house when we came to visit?* It was hard to believe that he was really my grandfather because my dad was a dark-complexioned man. My dad's mother had a dark complexion like my dad. That made a little sense in the reasoning behind the skin color variation in the family. The seven siblings on my dad's side of the family all varied in skin complexions, from dark to very light complexion. Even on my mother's side of the family, there was a rainbow of skin complexions as well. That is why it was difficult for me to process the notion of White superiority and why it was so difficult for some White Americans to treat Black Americans with dignity simply because of skin complexion. As far back as I can remember, I have been on trial and judged negatively because of my identifiable difference. Yet the justice system could not bring to trial known individuals who committed the act of murder. But neither I nor the Black community could give up hope for justice even though it appeared that justice had been delayed.

I could only imagine what the murderers must have thought. Based on their actions, they must have felt that they were above the law or under the power of sin. Their actions were notorious and cruel. Their hearts must have been filled with evil and envy because of the hatred that they showed by trying to destroy the House of Worship to seek revenge on Reverend Cross for allowing the civil rights leaders to hold the mass meeting at the church. There was no way that anyone holding to Christian morality could have carried out such a heinous crime. Life gives us choices. The choices we make about what to do or think shape our self-image, our personality, our view of the world, and our way of dealing with life. From that perspective, the choice made by the individuals who planted the bomb to cause destruction toward innocent Black Americans had to have been in a very dark place in their minds and hearts. Because of their Whiteness, they felt superior enough to eliminate individuals who did not possess the same Whiteness. Even living under the oppressive Jim Crow laws, I have witnessed that Black Americans have always shown a great level of humility. I was raised to be peaceful and considerate toward those who oppressed me and made me feel less than human. There had to be a divine Spirit dwelling within me to be my source of comfort and peace that helped me to control my thoughts and actions to not react negatively. History has shown that Black Americans have overcome circumstances that no other race of people had to endure.

When I was asking the why questions as a child, I was told to wait and be patient. Being patient was not my best character trait then, but I have learned that with patience I could relax and wait for the reward. Waiting and hoping for justice to prevail for the murder of my four friends weighed me down. I never expressed these feelings to anyone, because I just wanted the burden of doubt to go away. I kept trying to put the whole experience out of my mind. I could not fully comprehend the idea of casting all your burdens to the Lord. Through the hurt and disappointments, I would focus my attention on the melody of songs I learned as a child. One in particular is "Jesus loves me, this I know, for the Bible tells me so."

I remember wanting the year 1963 to hurry up and end because so much had happened that was not right or good. So many people had been hurt; and innocent lives were lost in the fight for freedom, equality, and justice for all. Then the news about Medgar Evers, a Mississippi civil rights leader, was assassinated on June 13, 1963, in his driveway because of his role for civil rights. I remember thinking, *What else could go wrong in the fight for justice and equality?* Then all the bombings in Birmingham happened—the Gaston Motel where King and the SCLC members stayed during the Birmingham campaign protest; the home of Attorney Author Shores, the home of King's brother, A. D. King; and then Sixteenth Street Baptist Church. But the evil and wickedness didn't end. On November 22, 1963, the president of the United States, John F. Kennedy, was assassinated in Dallas, Texas. The wicked White people of the South needed to turn from their wicked ways so that healing and justice could prevail. The Southland needed spiritual healing. I prayed for the day when White Americans would come to realize that discrimination and hatred were wrong and evil. Wrong and evil ways of thinking and feeling were not the way of life that the Creator of life intended for the people he created to live on his earth. It was beyond my understanding the complexity of how God created life, but it is clear that he did. That fact means that the Creator has authority over humanity—even the evil individuals who oppress Black Americans and kill innocent good White Americans who showed that they understand that truth.

During that point and time of my life, I felt that I had reached a dead end and the path was leading nowhere. One fact that my grandmothers and parents used to tell me was that only God knows what lies ahead. I had a choice before me. I chose to put my trust in God and continue to persevere with the hope that justice would prevail. The big picture about life was not in my hands. I had to believe that the future holds opportunities that I could ever hope or imagine for Black Americans. When John F. Kennedy was assassinated, I thought the hope for justice for Black Americans was dead. Kennedy had appealed to the conscience of Americans in his June 11, 1963, civil rights address to the public over national television and radio to stop and examine their conscience about the growing moral crisis in America's race relations. He reminded Americans that the United States was founded by individuals of many nations and backgrounds and on the principle that all are created equal and that the rights of every individual are diminished when the rights of one individual are threatened. As Americans, we should be committed to a worldwide struggle to promote and protect the rights of every citizen. Kennedy went on to say that it ought to be possible for every American to enjoy the privileges of being an American without regard to his race or his skin color. But this was not the case! Issues regarding segregation and discrimination existed in every city, in every State of the Union which produced a rising tide of discontent that threatened the public safety of the nation. Kennedy's message also pointed out that Americans were confronted with a moral issue that was as old as the Scriptures and as clear as the United States Constitution. The heart of the question was whether all Americans were to be afforded equal rights and equal opportunities. Kennedy continued with an appeal to Congress to pass legislation to end segregation in all public facilities and make a commitment to the proposition that racism had no place in American life or the law. Then five months after Kennedy addressed the nation and Congress, he was assassinated! When good White people show that they have a conscience and empathy for all Americans, they lose their life just like Black Americans. What was wrong with the people in this nation? "We the people."

Witnessing segregation and discrimination from a front-row seat made hope for justice and equality a heavy burden to carry. One hundred years had passed since President Lincoln freed the slaves; and Black Americans were not yet freed from the bonds of injustice, social, and economic oppression. I often wondered, How could most White Americans say that this is the land of the free when all its citizens are not free? The old code of equality under the law commands for every wrong, a remedy. At the same time, when wrongs were inflicted on Black Americans, there were no remedies from the law. All the events that took place in Birmingham and elsewhere in the

Southland were cries for equality and justice. The individuals governing the city of Birmingham and the state of Alabama chose to ignore the cries. Ignoring the cries brought about violence that caused fear, shame, and sorrow to the city.

There were times when I looked in the mirror and wondered why God gave me and other Black Americans a skin color that caused us to endure so much injustice and oppression. Then there were times I felt like I was lost in the wilderness all alone with nowhere to go even though I had parents who loved me and did their best to shield and protect me from the evils of segregation and discrimination. However, I could see the real truth unfolding before me. I did not like what I was seeing, but I was powerless. A future of equality and justice for all was a dream that I thought would never come true for Black Americans—because justice is about changing the connections that link us together and, from what I had witnessed and observed, most Southern White Americans did not want to be linked together with Black Americans.

My American history studies reminded me that Black Americans have been terrorized in America, mainly in the South, since the Compromise of 1877 and the collapse of Republican control in state government. Followed by a period when Southern-White-dominated state legislatures called Redeemers enacted Jim Crow laws and disenfranchised most Blacks and many poor Whites. A combination of constitutional amendments and electoral laws played a major role in imposing the system of White supremacy and second-class citizenship for Black Americans and poor Whites. With all the terrorism invoked on Black Americans, I often wondered what White Americans feared about our presence in America, especially since an African American slave named James Armistead played a large part in making possible the 1781 Yorktown victory, which established the United States as an independent nation. There are too many other contributions to mention that Black Americans made to make this nation a great place for all citizens. These were the big questions in my mind then! Why couldn't White Americans see all people as human beings, children of the *divine Creator*? Why couldn't they focus on the content of our character and cherish our differences? Spiritually, we are all connected. We all breathe the same air that is connected to the same source. When we learn to honor the differences and appreciate the mix, the hope for justice will be possible. There are infinite resources on this earth for everyone to achieve the American dream. In spite of these infinite resources, a few selfish individuals were not open to the idea of sharing. Greed and evil wills created a state of mind to oppress and exclude Black Americans. At a time when unity was so desperately needed in Birmingham, the basic philosophical differences placed the Black and White communities on opposite poles. Scripture tells us that God does not favor one race of people over another. God's Son died on the Cross for our sins over two thousand years ago. However, since his death, humanity is still fighting against coming together as one people as the human race regardless of skin color. The wall of injustice still prevails. When humanity begins the process of chipping away the injustice wall, the balance of justice for all citizens in Birmingham and the world can exist.

Months passed, and the justice department was unable to bring anyone to trial for bombing the church, so the scales of justice remained unbalanced. Made the cloud of fear continue to linger in the air. When the church reopened for service on June 7, 1964, I felt a little reluctant and anxious about going back inside the building where my life almost ended. I believed that my life and the other survivors were spared to grow our faith and character. Prior to the reopening of the church, I was given the opportunity to fly to California with my mother to represent the church as one of the survivors in the "Easter Freedom Parade Rally" in Sacramento that was sponsored by the Stars for Freedom Organization. Our flight plans required that we travel to Dallas, Texas, to make a connecting flight from there to Los Angeles, California. When we boarded the plane in Dallas, I was ecstatic to learn that Charles Evers, the brother of slain civil rights activist Medgar Evers, was on the plane headed to California. I did not know that he was going to California to participate in the same event. When the plane landed, we were met by Attorney Thomas G. Neusom, spokesman for Stars for Freedom; Sharon Parks, a junior college student chosen "Miss Freedom" for the

Easter Rally, along with her court; and news reporters who took our pictures and interviewed both of us.

Charles Evers told the reporters that he had received threats before he left Mississippi, that he would be killed in California if he participated in the freedom rally. Evers also said that he and his brother Medgar always agreed not to worry about death threats because they felt that they would rather die for a cause than die for nothing. When the reporter interviewed me, I was so nervous; but I did manage to say that I participated in the Children's Crusade March, I did not get injured by the water from the fire hoses, nor was I attacked by the vicious dogs, and I only received a few bruises and minor cuts from glass as I was making my escape from the church after the bomb exploded.

On that Easter Sunday afternoon during the Stars for Freedom parade, while I was riding in the White convertible Cadillac with Miss Freedom and her court, I thought, *This must be a dream*, as we slowly rode past all the well-wishers who were waving at us. That parade was an awesome experience for a little unknown "Colored girl" from Birmingham, Alabama. That moment made me feel very special. Living in a world made dark by injustice and racism required faith, courage, and a strong spiritual barrier. I had to believe that holding onto faith in all life circumstances would lead to new possibilities. I had to learn how to adapt to life's changes and plant positive thoughts in my mind that judgment day would come for the individuals who bombed the church. I had to believe that they could not get away with evil and the time for justice was just around the corner. I firmly believed that the way you treat others has a boomerang effect. Punishment for all acts of anger, envy, and hatred toward Black Americans would come to an end in due time according to divine order. The when and how were not in my control.

There was no doubt that humanity needed to be restored from spiritual darkness. The long-standing hostility against Black Americans needed to end. Humanity needed to be transformed with a new spirit of love and peace. I understand that change can be very difficult for most humans. But holding onto hatred, discrimination, and envy toward Black Americans keeps humanity in a place where peace, love, and justice cannot prevail. I believe that if humanity could release the past and move forward to a better tomorrow, then race and skin color will not be a barrier to justice and equality.

The summer of 1964 was the first summer since 1952 that my family did not travel to Washington, DC. The experience of spending my summer in the city of fear, sorrow, and shame was filled with apprehension. I was used to life in Washington, DC, during the summer months. Even though the Jim Crow laws had been abolished from a visible standpoint, there were limited social and cultural activities for Black American teenagers to experience. Birmingham did not have neoclassical monuments and buildings to visit. There were no iconic museums and performing-arts venues. There was no Rock Creek Park with trails to take hikes and just enjoy the outdoor recreation of walking through the West Potomac Park along the Potomac River. However, I was looking forward to the opportunity to attend Vacation Bible School and learn how I could be more honorable and loving toward everyone according to the teachings of Christ. Clearly, in the eyes of our White-dominated society, I was invisible, and I often felt invisible even though I knew that I coexisted on earth with billions of people. I had to frequently remind myself that I was not being short-changed and whatever I needed would be provided to help me accomplish my goals and aspirations to be successful. I also started to realize that every major change in life brings challenges.

I am sure that the pressure of transition on the part of some White Americans to dissolve White supremacy would bring about major changes in their lives and their ways of thinking and believing how society should function. From the beginning of time, our Creator gave us instructions on how we should live on earth so that peace, tranquility, and safety would prevail for all of God's creations. But the laws that were in place to impose barriers on the lives of Black Americans were a form of disobedience to the will of God. Yet at the same time, those individuals who imposed the laws that placed barriers on the lives of Black Americans claim to know God. Another big question comes to mind: *How can someone claim to know God and not show true love to everyone?*

Aside from attending Vacation Bible School and reading books, I had no idea what else to do for entertainment in Birmingham. During the summer months, my dance class sessions were on break. Our summertimes in Washington, DC, were always planned out from the time we arrived until it was time for us to return to Birmingham. I felt out of place in my hometown. My mother, not knowing how to drive, placed limits on the places we could go.

Ann had a boyfriend who had a car, but she didn't like it when Mother insisted that I go with them on some of their dates. Our mother had very strict rules. Ann told me that she couldn't wait to leave home so that she could be more independent. She was accepted to attend Clark College, now Clark Atlanta University in Atlanta, Georgia, at the end of August 1964. I imagine the money that my dad had to spend for us to travel to DC was needed to help pay for her school expenses. She had received a full scholarship to attend Tougaloo College in Mississippi. But she told my parents under no circumstances did she want to go anywhere in Mississippi. She reminded them that living in Birmingham was bad enough. Going further south was out of the question. I was definitely on my sister's side regarding her choice not to go further south. I had already made it clear to my parents that when I finished high school, I did not want to attend college in Alabama or anywhere south of Alabama. Our parents were not well-off, but they made a promise to Ann and me that we could go to the college of our choice if we maintained high academic standards throughout elementary and high school.

Ann and I were very close growing up, but we never talked about attending the same college after we finished high school. My goal was to become a prima ballerina. Even though my dad was always telling me that I needed to have a backup plan and make sure I kept my grades in good standing, I believe my dad was trying to tell me that my dream of being a ballerina on the world's stage might not be possible for a little "Colored girl" from Birmingham, Alabama. I was somewhat disappointed that my dad was not supportive of my dream. I never got a lead part, regardless of how well I executed the routine when we were preparing for our dance recitals. I did not have long flowing hair and a light skin complexion. Which was the look that all ballerinas had. My dad always told me that I was his beautiful baby girl. I had a good figure and great coordination. So I tried not to let negative thoughts place limits on my ability to live the life I dreamed. I took an honest look at what I believed about myself and the guidance from my parents and decided to sweep false and destructive thoughts out of my mind and move toward a dream that might be more realistic from where I stood. I loved moving my body to the sound of jazz and classical music. When my ears heard and my body moved with the rhythm, I was able to escape and cope with the environment and the difficult situations. I was able to take my mind and thoughts to a place that would soothe my soul.

Attending Vacation Bible School that summer allowed me to embrace my spiritual identity and revel in true freedom knowing that I was a beautiful girl. Studying the scriptures helped reveal to me that I am a beautiful being created in the image and likeness of God. As I ascended into my new understanding of myself, I was able to see life from a limitless perspective and embrace my spiritual truth. I learned that I had to be in charge of my reality and know my truth. However, living in Birmingham made it hard to keep a continual flow of positive ideas about the future. My belief in justice was tinged with doubt and suspicion because of the integrity of the people who were in positions of leadership. Even though I was living in an unjust world, I decided to hold firm to my faith.

I recognized a small piece of political justice that came about when President Lyndon Johnson signed into law on July 2, 1964, the Civil Rights Act. The act had initially been drawn up by President Kennedy's administration. Congress filibustered for seventy-five days by die-hard Southerners before it became a law. That action by Congress lifted some of the spiritual darkness in our nation. The Civil Rights Act applied to the entire nation; it prohibited racial discrimination in employment and allowed access to all public places to all citizens. Thanks to the Birmingham campaign for opening the eyes of the world to the evils of segregation, that move became the most important chapter in the nonviolence Civil Rights Movement.

Passing the Civil Rights Act was a step in the right direction that opened the doors to further progress. It did not end discrimination even though the act outlawed discrimination based on race, color, religion, sex, or national origin. And the act did not establish justice for the bombing of the church. The murderers had not been brought to trial. Our justice system failed in its attempt to ascertain that the individuals responsible for bombing the church were liable for the death of the four young girls. They died a wrongful and unjustifiable death. But if we can look at death as a prerequisite for change and accept death as a meaningful new beginning, then the death of the four young girls would not have been in vain, and humanity can move from spiritual darkness into the light of change.

Through all the years of suffering and discouragement that had threatened the lives of Black Americans, as a race of people, we somehow did not lose our confidence in future hope for salvation. I truly believed there was hope for the future because the Jesus that I learned about in Vacation Bible School is an anchor for our souls. This means that hope for the future cannot and will not be shaken loose (Hebrews 6:19–20). Believing the promises of an unchanging and trustworthy God, I believed that hope for justice would roll down like a mighty stream.

Five months and eight days later, the Civil Rights Act became law. Another step toward lifting spiritual darkness from the nation occurred on December 10, 1964. Dr. Martin Luther King Jr. was awarded and accepted the Nobel Peace Prize for advocating a policy of nonviolence during the Birmingham campaign. In spite of all the good that was unfolding, fifteen months had passed, and still there was no justice for the church bombing. My faith in hope for justice was still being challenged. I prayed that justice would not be uprooted like a fallen tree. I did not understand how the justice system could be so blinded by their acts of injustice to a crime of murder toward innocent children. Was it a measure of punishment toward the children who took part in the nonviolent Children Crusade protest? I surely did not want to believe that was the case, because the children who took part in the crusade were fighting for equality and justice, and for the opportunity to share the American dream with dignity and respect. I believe that every human being should be allowed the opportunity to know that they are appreciated and welcomed simply for being who they are and regardless of the color of their skin.

From my perspective, and I am sure others might share my view, the cloud of spiritual darkness in Birmingham would not be completely lifted until justice for the murder of the four innocent girls had prevailed. For as far back as I can remember, society's standard of judging others had been based solely on appearances and race. Birmingham and the nation desperately needed a revival of justice and fairness that would change the hearts of the selfish individuals who refused to give justice to the oppressed. The big question that faced Birmingham and the nation was, *How can the struggle for justice be accomplished?* It was obviously clear to America during the Civil Rights Movement protest that the approach to justice should be non-violence. Violence was not the way—even though history has shown that violence has always been invoked toward Black Americans for their efforts after the end of slavery to achieve justice and equality. Scripture tells us that there is no law of fairness or justice that is higher and more absolute than God and that God himself is the standard of justice. This gave me hope to believe that, in due time, judgment would come to the individuals who bombed the church.

My hope for quick justice would help to bring closure for the senseless and unjust murders. I believed that faith would give me the ability to continue to hope and persevere so that the unforgettable day that shamed the nation would not be a memory that would affect my life. The church bombing event happened within seconds, but the memory of those seconds will live forever in my mind. I have heard the saying that life is like a camera and all we need to do is focus on what's important and capture the good times, develop from the negatives, and if things don't work out, just take another shot. But for Addie, Carol, Cynthia, and Denise, the bombing moment didn't work out for them; and they will no longer be able to focus on what's important and capture the good times and develop from the negatives. They will not be able to take another shot at life.

Those of us who survived the church bombing were given another shot at life to focus on how we would develop from that negative event and help bring about change. In due time, the sorrow, the hatred, and the shame in the city of Birmingham and the nation will no longer be a factor. I was ready to embrace the new changes that would come out of that heinous and vicious crime. I believe as a person of faith that the light of hope for justice will eventually shine.

Keeping an optimistic view about the judicial system, the hope for justice may not be a remote idea. Sometimes, it was hard not to focus on the negative rather than on the ultimate goal. But that meant giving up the fight for equality and justice. I believed in the strategic plans of the nonviolence movement that we would overcome someday. And one day, we will all have to stand before judgment and receive whatever we deserve for the good or evil that we have done.

Medgar Evers' Brother Tells of Death Threat

Kin, Here for 'Easter Freedom Parade,' Dismisses Phone Call as Work of 'Crank'

BY PAUL WEEKS
Times Staff Writer

A telephoned threat that he would "be killed in California" was made to Charles Evers, brother of the slain Medgar Evers, before he left Mississippi to attend a rally here, he disclosed Friday.

Evers, who succeeded his brother as Mississippi field secretary for the NAACP, dismissed the threat as "just another crank call."

He flew here to participate in an "Easter Freedom Parade" at 1 p.m. Sunday, followed by a "Freedom Festival" of performers at 3 p.m. at the Sports Arena.

Slain on June 12

Medgar Evers was fatally shot June 12. Byron de La Beckwith, 43, his accused assassin, is scheduled to stand a second trial beginning April 6. The first trial ended when the all-white jury failed to agree on a verdict.

"Medgar and I always agreed we could never worry about death threats," the brother Charles said on his arrival here. "We both felt we'd rather die for a cause than to die for nothing—and if it's going to happen to you, it's going to happen."

Charles Evers said the latest death threat call was from a man who pointed out that de La Beckwith was born a Californian.

"We're going to let California kill you, too," he quoted the caller as saying.

The brother refused to comment on de La Beckwith's first trial while the second one is still pending.

He said Medgar's wife, Myrlie, had flown here Thursday.

"We don't fly together," he said. "We don't want to give anyone an opportunity like that," he added.

Get on Plane

Aboard the same plane with Charles Evers, however, was Ethel Madison, 15-year-old Birmingham school-girl who was cut by flying glass in the same Birmingham church bomb blast that killed four Negro girls in September. Ethel was accompanied by her mother, Mrs. Annie A. Madison.

Attorney Thomas G. Neusom, spokesman for Stars for Freedom, who greeted the visitors, said Ethel will be given a $500 college scholarship for the efforts she is making in the civil rights movement.

In answer to a question, Ethel said she had marched in civil rights demonstrations before the bombing incident, "but unlike most of the other kids, I didn't ever get put in jail," she said.

The girl said, however, she is "willing to go to jail" if it should come to that in the civil rights movement.

Negroes in Mississippi, Charles Evers said, are "more determined than ever to become free" since his brother's death, and "want the world to know that to destroy one man doesn't destroy a movement."

The "drive for freedom" will go on regardless of whether the civil rights bill passes Congress, he said. Should it fail, however, he said, hate groups may get more followers in the South.

Sharon Parks, junior college student chosen "Miss Freedom" for the Easter rally, greeted the visitors with her court.

Sacramento Plan

Another civil rights action is planned for today in an "Easter-Passover Walk and Rally" starting at 12:30 p.m. at Figueroa St. and Santa Barbara Ave., and moving to the bandshell at South Park. Dr. Linus Pauling, Nobel prize winner, will be chairman of the meeting.

The United Civil Rights Committee, meanwhile, announced a "leadership mobilization" in Sacramento at 9:30 a.m. Tuesday to urge legislators to put off the vote on the housing initiative until the November ballot.

The initiative, by constitutional amendment, would forbid anti-discriminatory legislation such as the Rumford Housing Act.

A nationwide closed-circuit television fund-raising program for the NAACP was also announced Friday. It is set for May 14 on the 10th anniversary of the U.S. Supreme Court's outlawing of school segregation.

To be broadcast from Los Angeles and New York, the show will be tied in with 45 cities, with a fund-raising goal of $1 million to be earmarked for bail bonds for persons arrested in demonstrations.

Me with Megan Evers' brother after deplaning in California to take part in the Easter Freedom Parade.

Chapter 5

Let them turn away from evil and do good;
let them seek peace and pursue it.

—1 Peter 3:11

The idea of peace and exactly how it played such an important role in my future dreams were not at the forefront of my mind during my early years. But as I got older and noticed how the world and especially the city of Birmingham produced fear and danger, I wondered how I was going to find peace of mind, let alone seek and pursue peace. After the Civil Rights Movement, I tried to envision Birmingham as a place where all people could live harmoniously and peacefully regardless of our race or the color of our skin. I did not want to believe that human beings preferred doing evil over doing good. I believe that as the citizens of Birmingham learn how to build good relationships and celebrate our differences—the spice that makes us unique and interesting—we could then seek peace and pursue it.

For me to achieve the peace that I needed to continue to move forward, I had to find peace in my heart to forgive those who caused me to feel fearful. And believe that I was not good enough. I grew up in a peaceful and loving home. I never heard my parents raise their voices at each other. And they did not allow Ann and me to say ugly words or disrespect our individual views. They believed that peace in the home could spread peace to the community and throughout the nation, so then there would be no room for conflict. But I know that making peace is hard work. And it has to be the ultimate goal for our nation, especially in the Southlands and even beyond the borders. According to scripture, peace is an instrument that flows within each of us. Imagine a world with thoughts of peace flowing through everyone's heart. Then there would be no room for evil thoughts and actions.

Believing that we are all part of the same spirit means that we were created to support one another through the storms of life. We were created by the Creator to be a family firmly bound together by our roots, which means that we should respect the dignity and worth of everyone. Segregation is morally wrong and sinful. So another question that boggled my mind was this: How would the city of Birmingham and the nation find a way to overcome the morally wrong and sinful behavior of segregation, discrimination, and unjust laws? It was very clear that the evil forces needed to be purged from society and replaced with a spirit of humility, selflessness, compassion, and love for all mankind. For the good of our nation, we needed to move in a new direction—a direction of peace.

My mind was so boggled during that period of my life. I had so many questions and concerns. I thought about issues related to personal differences. How do we let go of our personal differences and become a nation centered in love and treating others with kindness, dignity, and respect without regard to race, color, religion, or national origin? Honoring diversity brings about peace to our communities, nation, and the world. Ending the stigma of racism could help eliminate the spiritual darkness from Birmingham and other parts of the Southland and our nation. Because it was clear that the resistance to civil rights is wrong.

The notion that some people are inherently better than others because of skin color is wrong. There was so much wrong in our society before the Civil Rights Movement that many White Americans just turned a blind eye to because it did not affect them directly. They seemed blind to what was right. When I think about what Scripture tells us about the time before the flood, God had observed the extent of human wickedness and saw that everything humanity thought or imagined was consistently and totally evil. In the city of Birmingham and all over the Southlands, evil acts were so out of control during the 1960s that the hope for peace in Birmingham and the entire state of Alabama rested in the hearts of leaders whose hearts seemed to be hardened against doing what was right for justice and peace. The true hope for peace for Birmingham and the world could come about if the individual leaders learn to think, speak, and act peacefully.

When the nonviolent demonstrators in Selma, Alabama, were attacked by the state troopers with clubs and tear gas on March 7, 1965, during their march for the voting rights campaign from Selma to Montgomery, the state capital of Alabama, I could not believe what I saw on national television. I thought, How many more evil acts and suffering can evil White Americans invoke on Black Americans? The Alabama State troopers were cheered on by evil White onlookers as they chased the demonstrators and beat them like they were animals. Those acts of evil led me to believe that most Southern White Americans did not have a conscience or soul. Thankfully, after that horrible scene, President Johnson addressed the US Congress on national television to speak to the conscience of the law enforcers who were acting unlawfully toward peaceful marchers. He said, and I quote, "Their cause must be our cause, too, because it is not just the 'Negroes,' but really it is all of us who must overcome the crippling legacy of bigotry and injustice." That message gave me a glimmer of hope in my heart for some peace to prevail. Even though his wording was not tasteful to my ears. "Their cause!" Johnson signed the Voting Rights Act of 1965. The act gave Americans, especially Black Americans, hope and peace that were long overdue. The act opened the door for Black Americans to feel whole as human beings. The right to vote was the most powerful instrument ever devised by man to break down injustice and destroy the terrible walls that imprison us because of our differences.

I was looking forward to leaving Birmingham after graduating from high school in May 1965. I wanted to get as far away from the South as possible. Since my dream to become a ballerina on the world's stage did not work in my favor and my plans to attend Howard University in Washington, DC, I decided to attend Tennessee A & I State University (renamed Tennessee State University in 1968) in Nashville, Tennessee, which was my third choice. I knew Nashville was a Southern state; but Nashville was known to be one of the most refined and educated cities of the South. Nashville was considered to be the "Athens of the South" because of its educational system. But the pattern of racial exclusiveness prevailed in Nashville, just like it did in all other Southern cities. Protests for civil rights occurred in Nashville about three years before the protests began in Birmingham. That put Nashville a few steps ahead of Birmingham with regards to race relations. The Nashville Christian Leadership Conference (NCLC) under the leadership of Reverend Kelly Miller Smith led a movement to desegregate downtown Nashville. Students from Fisk University, Tennessee A & I State University, Meharry Medical College, and American Baptist Theological Seminary were trained to participate in the sit-in demonstrations and launch their first full-scale sit-in on February 13, 1960. After three months of sit-ins and racial violence, the demonstrations organized by Fisk student leader Diane Nash marched to Nashville's city hall to confront Mayor Ben West. On May 10, 1960, the mayor conceded to the protestors and told them that he felt that segregation was wrong, and Nashville became the first major Southern city to begin desegregating its public facilities.

Although Black Americans had access to public facilities, the city was still segregated just like Birmingham. When I arrived in Nashville at the end of August 1965, I discovered that Tennessee State University, Fisk University, and Meharry Medical College were all located within proximity to each other in the Black section of town. After touring the city of Nashville, I was somewhat disappointed to see the vast difference on the side of town where the Black colleges are located compared to where Vanderbilt University, Belmont College, and Lipscomb University were located. The distribution of wealth was clearly obvious. The economic disparity was highly visible in Nashville, Tennessee, just like in Birmingham, Alabama. The campuses of the three Black colleges were nice, but the areas surrounding the campuses were not like the areas surrounding Vanderbilt, Belmont, and Lipscomb. Similar to Birmingham, the White-dominated society in Nashville clearly had the upper hand to economic wealth. I could clearly see that the struggle for justice and peace were not the only issues facing Black Americans; the struggle for economic equality through my eyes was a major issue. So I was boggled with the idea, How can there be peace and justice without economic equality?

The March on Washington in 1963 for jobs and freedom that attracted thousands of individuals from all around the world was an effort to convince the president and Congress to share the economic wealth with Black Americans. It was clearly obvious through my eyes that only small efforts had been made to create the American dream for all Americans. America is a nation of plenty. Being positioned between two great oceans with some of the greatest natural resources in the world makes it possible for all Americans to live without want. Yet Black Americans continued to be oppressed, which will keep America divided against herself. The Founding Fathers established this nation on the great principles of democracy at the time when Black Americans were slaves. Slavery has been abolished; yet as a Black American, sometimes, I felt like I was living in a desertlike place, trying to navigate my way with limited and restricted resources. My parents were able to pay our college tuition despite the oppression and economic disparity toward Black Americans. They never showed any signs of hardship while Ann and I were in college. But making the true American dream a reality for all mankind remained a challenge because America has not totally eliminated the last vestiges of segregation and discrimination. Segregation is both politically and economically unsound for a nation to achieve the justice and peace that hold truths to be self-evident that every individual is created equal. Issues related to segregation and discrimination needed to be solved before it's too late. The world is watching America. Humanity was being challenged to work on a plan to get rid of segregation and discrimination to make the American dream become a reality and make real the promises of a democracy. "We the People of the United States!" As I continue to hope that the American dream will be a reality, I truly believe that nonviolence is the way. The nonviolent philosophy of passive resistance is as old as the insights of "Jesus of Nazareth" and as modern as the techniques of Mohandas K. Gandhi when he led the struggle to help India gain independence from Great Britain. And under the leadership of Nelson Mandela, the apartheid revolution came to an end. Over the years, I have witnessed how

Black Americans could endure suffering and show love at the same time. Learning how to agree with one another is the road toward achieving peace. If we allow peace to reside in our hearts and minds, that same peace can spread so that segregation and discrimination will no longer clog our society, allowing complete peace to prevail.

To stay focused and think clearly while I was pursuing my educational goals, race relations needed to take a backseat in my mind. I had to suppress the evils of our society to my subconscious mind and shut the world out. Because not much had changed in both the White and Black communities since the Birmingham protest, the March on Washington and the Sixteenth Street Baptist Church bombing, other than making public facilities available to all citizens. However, my dreams for a better America remained. At seventeen years old, a first-year student in college, I never had the privilege of experiencing being employed other than helping my mother place the pattern pieces in the right order on the fabric and cutting the pieces out that would eventually become a garment made to perfection for the individual who had been measured. I did not expect to receive pay for this service, because I felt proud and honored to be able to help my mother. While growing up, Ann and I did not get an allowance for the chores that we did around the house. However, Mother would give us money for Sunday school and church. If we needed money for special events or activities, it was always available to us. We always had nice clothes and shoes to wear. Based on what I saw during our family travels and observing the lives of the privileged from watching some television shows and reading about in magazines, I could clearly see the inequality of wealth in our society. There were no television shows in the 1960s that featured Black families like the Cleaver family. Even though my family kind of mirrored the Cleaver family, I could still see and felt the inequity. So the "why" question was always in the back of my mind. I thought, *What can I do to acquire some of the wealth of this great nation?*

I knew that just acquiring a good job would not bring the kind of wealth that I saw in the privileged White communities. My father had a federal government job. And we certainly did not live a privileged life. Economic opportunities for young Black Americans did not appear to be on upward mobility during the mid-1960s even though the purpose of the March on Washington was to bring about shared prosperity, which had been at the heart of our nation's promise since its founding. Perhaps that promise did not include Black Americans! After all, our ancestors were brought here against their will. With that thought flowing through my mind, I wonder what was ahead for me after college. I was always told by my parents and led to believe that education is the tool needed to bargain with society to make a better life because knowledge determines the value of the job market. In spite of not coming from a privileged background and not having a bank account in my name, I went off to college with a certified check for my tuition and fees, room and board, and just enough cash in my possession to pay for my books and supplies and take care of incidental expenses.

Entering a historically Black university with a rich legacy gave me hope and courage to think that a better future could be ahead. Tennessee A & I State University was founded in 1912 for Negroes. The doors first opened to 247 students with an emphasis on agricultural and industrial occupations. In 1922, the school became a college and, in 1951, acquired university status. The university achieved full land-grant university status in 1958 that included the School of Agriculture and Home Economics, the graduate school, the Division of Extension and Continuing Education, and the Department of Aerospace Studies. The university's motto "Enter to learn; go forth to serve" engraved on a plaque on the wall in the administration building was a constant visible reminder of the charge before me and all the students enrolled.

While navigating through life as a college student majoring in pure mathematics, the struggle for justice, peace, and equality were still major issues in our society. I had high hopes that one day I would be able to contribute to society with the knowledge that I was gaining through some form of scientific research and development program. While justice, peace, and equality were still lingering issues in our society, I had to keep the faith that humility one day would be the guiding force in our society that would make things right and good for all mankind. However, at the same time, the future ahead seemed dark and uncertain for me. Black Americans were still fighting for civil rights. With my focus on mathematics, my knowledge and understanding of political science and the policies governing our political system were very limited. But I had deep concerns about the political issues that affected the well-being and lives of all Americans. Life as a full-time student kept me sheltered from most of the evil wills of our society, but I was not blind to the injustices that existed.

By the time I reached my senior year in college in 1968, justice still had not prevailed regarding the death of my four friends, yet another terrorist occurrence happened. Dr. Martin Luther King Jr.—the drum major for justice, peace, and righteousness—was assassinated. The violence against the innocent was still on a rampage in our society. The nonviolence campaign promoted by Dr. King was overshadowed by his death, which excited the kind of violence that he deplored all across the nation. However, Nashville maintained an atmosphere of some calm during that time by placing a curfew on the city. The students on all the Black campuses were not allowed to leave campus after sundown. The assassination of Dr. King struck the nation with intense concern that his strategy of nonviolence would come to an end. Although rioting took place in several major cities, nonviolence was the primary focus for most Black communities. My faith gave me the courage to believe that Black Americans had the perseverance to handle difficult situations with godly character. My faith also gave me the courage to believe that good would result when we endure difficulties with patience. However, without justice for all, there is no peace.

The struggle for peace over the past hundred years had been a clash against evil wills—the will to commit wrongful acts against humanity with no recourse, the will to hate because of differences, the will to discriminate and oppress because of differences. It was the evil will of the late FBI director J. Edgar Hoover to stop and shut down the church bombing investigation in 1968 in spite of the fact that the FBI agents had accumulated sufficient evidence against the suspects: Robert "Dynamite Bob" Chambliss, Thomas E. Blanton Jr., and Bobby Frank Cherry. Based upon the actions of Hoover, it was very clear that he did not have a conscience or compassion for Black Americans. His primary focus had been on harassing and trying to destroy the reputation of Dr. King.

The road toward freedom and equality leaves an ugly mark about America's society in my mind even though anti-Black violence had begun to decline. Black candidates were being elected to political offices, and some Southern White colleges and universities began to recruit Black students to enroll because of federal mandates. Despite the civil rights gains that were being made during the early and late 1960s, I could still see that racial discrimination and oppression were still significant factors in America's society. The distribution of the nation's wealth and income disparity appeared to be moving toward a greater inequity, which was a clear indication that the evil wills were still working to discriminate and continue oppression. In spite of the fact that President Johnson had declared a war on poverty and Dr. King had initiated the Poor People's Campaign before he was assassinated, the inequity of wealth was a real social issue then and even today.

While all the evil wills were still factors in our society, I had to find a way to focus on what I needed to do to have a piece of the glory of the American dream. This required me to suppress the ugly reminders of the past. I was not sure how to boast in suffering—even though Scripture tells me that suffering produces endurance, endurance produces character, character produces hope, and hope does not disappoint. That kind of hope was hard for me to digest during that period in my life. I was just beginning to realize that life is unpredictable and there would be countless things that would occur in the future that I would never know with certainty. But what I did know and believe was that there is a power greater and more powerful than all of us who knows all and loves us all deeply. Knowing that fact, I could feel some sense of peace.

During my college years, I did not talk about what it was like growing up in Birmingham. Most people had such a grim view of the city because of what they heard and saw in the media during the Civil Rights Movement. I never mentioned that I was in the church when the bomb exploded and the conservation I had with the four girls. I thought, if I did not talk about the event, the pain and hurt would stay suppressed in my subconscious and slowly be lifted from my mind. I wanted to be able to embrace the future with an open mind that peace and justice would prevail for everyone one day. However, I had problems visualizing where I was going to fit into the big scheme of life. I was just an unknown shy Black American teenage girl from Birmingham, Alabama, with high hopes and dreams to make a contribution toward scientific research with my mathematical knowledge. I also had a burning desire to become an activist for peace and justice. I had a willing spirit to speak out against injustice and inequality in our society but was not sure how to make my voice heard. I was not blessed with the speaking ability to capture and lure the ears and hearts of others, but I was willing to be a warrior for truth and justice. I joined the NAACP Nashville branch as a youth member to help support the organization in the defense of civil rights. As a youth member, I felt that by belonging to an organization dedicated to social justice and equality for all people, I could make some kind of contribution to help bring about change. I did not have a specific role to play as a member. However, I was ready to serve and work for the cause, volunteering for community service.

The social upheavals during the sixties had a profound effect on my attitude in relation to my future opportunities. Studying the liberal arts gave me the general knowledge of language, history, and literature which helped to develop my intellectual capacity to reason and make judgments. Studying mathematics and science was designed to develop my specific skills for my profession, in addition to developing my critical thinking skills and higher-order problem-solving skills. But even with studying the liberal arts and sciences, I was well aware that the foreseeable future may not work in my favor. Even though the Civil Rights Movement challenged the existing social and political structure to make changes so that all eligible citizens have an equal say in the decisions that affect their lives, the privileged Whites were trying to hold onto what they held most dear—power.

Before I completed my coursework to earn my bachelor's degree, I visited the Career Development Center on campus to seek out the job opportunities that were available for an individual with a major in mathematics other than teaching high school, which I would not be able to do at that time, because I did not take the courses required to get a certificate in secondary education. All of my minor coursework was in mathematics. My dad wanted me to follow in his footsteps and get a job with the federal government. Because of his encouragement and my trust in his judgment, I took the civil service exam to get my name on the federal government's job roster—even though my dreams were not to be stuck in some office or room figuring out an algorithm to solve a problem. Initially, I was interested in doing scientific research that required a background in mathematics. But as I navigated my way through my outlined curriculum, my brain was stretched to the limit. I started to second-guess myself. And what I was experiencing during my search for jobs through the Career Development Center seemed uncertain.

Because of the system of White supremacy, it was frustrating for young Black Americans like me in the late 1960s with regards to finding suitable work. Fair treatment was not on the table. The unemployment rate among educated Black Americans was much higher than the unemployment rate for educated White Americans. President Johnson had signed the Civil Rights Act of 1968 (Fair Housing Act) on April 11, 1968, which had no impact on employment for Black Americans. Without employment, finding suitable housing would be virtually impossible. Our nation was facing an economic recession in addition to dealing with the unpopular war being forged in Vietnam. The visible barriers of racism were gone. But the underlying systemic barriers were still there. Earning a degree from a historically Black institution would not put me on the same playing field as a White graduate with the same degree.

I was so puzzled by life that I made a decision that my parents were not happy about. I got married without their permission to a man I had only known for six months. I was twenty years old but not legally an adult in the eyes of the law in the state of Tennessee. My future husband, William Van Buren, and I, along with two of my classmates, Cynthia Garrett and Cherrie Gilkey, crossed the state line back into Alabama to get the marriage license and recited our vows to the Justice of Peace on November 21, 1968. I took this leap of faith because after graduation I did not want to go back to Birmingham, Alabama, if I didn't find employment after graduation in Nashville or with the federal government. And I couldn't picture my life in Washington, DC, a place which I once admired and could escape from the evil wills of segregation in the South. I thought getting married was my only option. I caught the bridal bouquet at Ann's wedding in August 1968. She had just graduated from Clark College with a degree to teach high school mathematics and also a contract to teach with the Atlanta school system in September 1968. She had her life all mapped out so that she would not have to return to Birmingham. Catching her bridal bouquet was an indication to me that I was next in line to take the plunge, although I had no plans for marriage on my mind that day. I met William in June of 1968 when I was walking across the campus on my way back to my dorm room after class. He took me to meet his mother on our first date. William came from a good family. His father, who was deceased when we met, had been a prominent dentist in Clarksville and Nashville, Tennessee. William was the fourth child of seven siblings. His oldest sister, Betty, was a professor in the Speech and Drama Department at Tennessee State University and an adjunct professor at Fisk University. From what I could see during our courtship, his upbringing was kind of similar to mine. His mother was a stay-at-home mom like my mother, who loved her children dearly. William was twenty-two and still living at home with his mother and his three younger siblings—Albretta, Sherman, and Ronnie. I did not realize until after I took the plunge that William did not have his head focused in the right direction. I kept the marriage a secret from my parents until I finished my college work so that they would continue to pay my tuition. William was not financially able to pay my tuition, which should have turned on the yellow light in my head before I took the leap. When my parents finally learned that I was married, my dad was devastated. He could not believe his baby girl married a man without his approval and blessings. My mother acted as if she was okay with the union. After the shock of my eloping wore off, our families became one.

I completed my coursework for the bachelor of science degree in mathematics in December of 1969 and began my search for employment. Unlike Ann, who had a contract to teach before she graduated, I thought and believed that I would not have any problems finding employment with my credentials. My name was on the federal government's job roster, but I never received a reply for an interview for any of the positions for which I submitted my résumé. My visits to the Career Development Center on campus only gave me leads to jobs in my field out of the state of Tennessee, and my husband didn't want to leave his beloved hometown, and he also needed to finish his college coursework. Those constraints led me to employment unrelated to my intellectual knowledge and skills.

I applied for a position with the state of Tennessee on the advice of my husband's sister, Virgie, who worked in the governor's office at the time. She informed me that there were three vacancies for research assistance with the legislative division within the comptroller's office. So I applied for one of the three positions. When I sat for the interview, I was told that the positions had already been filled and the only vacancy that they could offer me at that time was an account clerk's position. That position did not require a bachelor's degree but required clerical skills which I did not have. Obviously, the interviewer did not want me to have the position that I was clearly qualified to perform based on my credentials for no reason other than I was a Black American and did not belong there. Perhaps, as I mentioned earlier, my degree from a Black university did not carry the same weight as a degree from a White university, even though Tennessee State University had full land-grant status just like the other state schools under the Tennessee Board of Regents.

I left the job interview feeling crushed and degraded. After spending four long years burning the midnight oil learning how to find the area under the curve; finding the limit of functions if they exist; evaluating derivatives and integrals; analyzing differential equations; and studying the theory of numbers, complex variables and analysis, advanced calculus, etc., just to mention the tip of the iceberg, the only position I was qualified to perform in the eyes of the White power structure was a menial position that required typing skills, which were not part of my course of studies. My sense of hope for employment was shaken. I was devastated to the core. Neither my education nor my parents had prepared me for that kind of rejection. I had great expectations for the future because I believed that the March on Washington had made an impact toward expanding opportunities for Black Americans to gain meaningful employment. I guess the situation with the job position was a trial that I had to endure in life to test my faith. In order to survive the storm of injustice and discrimination, I had to remain strong through that trial and find a way to fight against the injustice with the tiny rippling of hope left in my soul to sweep down the mighty walls of oppression and resistance.

That period of my life made me think that hope for justice and equality seemed scarce. My sister-in-law Virgie encouraged me to take the account clerk position to get my foot in the door and reapply for the research assistant's position again at a later date. I thought that higher education training was the first step to getting your foot in the door for a position that fits your credentials. I told my husband and sister-in-law that I would rather be a career student than work in a dead-end job with no guarantee of moving to a higher level. I was in a situation where I could not control what was happening. I was twenty-one years old with a college degree but no specific job skill according to the employment system. I stopped and asked myself the question, Did I waste four years learning how to apply critical thinking skills to solve real-world problems and end up at a roadblock with nowhere to go? Racism and job discrimination smacked me dead in the face. My eyes were opened to the realization that I lived in a world that didn't value me as a totally whole individual. And I did not have a strategic place in the American idea.

After considering Virgie's advice, I took the position because I needed to be employed for my self-worth. Being productive was important and necessary to life. After being on the job for three weeks, hunting and pecking my way around on the keyboard of the IBM electric typewriter to type invoices for the state legislators to receive their paychecks, my White supervisor who did not have a college degree suggested that I take a typing class through the state's educational training program to improve my typing skills. I felt so insulted. Tears rolled down my face like a mighty stream. I had just completed four years of rigorous studies in mathematics to earn a bachelor's degree. During the interview, I made it clear that I didn't have any typing skills and was hired in spite of. My supervisor did not understand why I was crying. He expressed to me that I was not being fired, but I was so hurt that I didn't care if I had been fired. My future aspirations had nothing to do with clerical skills. I was the only Black person working in that division of the state government other than the custodial workers. I wanted them to fire me so that I could file a discrimination lawsuit against the state of Tennessee. I suppose that was the reason my supervisor offered the training option rather than let me go. I tried very hard not to look at the situation as hopeless, but I felt persecuted from every angle.

After six weeks of training in the typing class, my typing speed improved to about fifteen to twenty words a minute. We all have our individual gifts. Mastering how to use the IBM electric typewriter was not mine. The typing instructor took pity on me and gave me the certificate stating that I had completed the training requirement although we were required to gain a speed of thirty to forty words a minute to complete the course requirements. Knowing that I did not meet the required typing speed for the certificate, I didn't want to take the certificate, because I take the learning process seriously. The instructor told me that my speed would get better with time. However, I never mastered the skills to make the typewriter talk like the typing instructor. God gave me the gift to understand complex mathematical concepts.

Twelve months had passed on the job, and I discovered that two of the three positions for research assistant were still vacant, although I was told during my first interview that all the positions had been filled. Before I decided to reapply, I sought to find the individual who had been hired to fill one of the positions. I discovered that the individual was a White female who had graduated from the University of Tennessee with a degree in political science. She was very friendly toward me and very open to sharing her duties and responsibilities. Her office was furnished with a nice mahogany desk with a reclining chair surrounded with shelves of books and briefs. When I told her that I had a degree in mathematics, she looked surprised after I told her that I was an account clerk. When I told her that I was told that the research assistant positions were all filled, she had a puzzled look on her face. So I reapplied for the position. The division of state government where I worked gave me access to see all the state vacancies that were not available to the public. I had access to the payroll information for every employee who worked within the state comptroller's office including the state legislators. I was told by the same interviewer who interviewed me twelve months earlier that those positions did not actually exist and that they were listed only for auditing purposes. The yellow light bulb came on in my head, and I was able to read between the lines. Those positions were not available to be filled by Black Americans. I was not sure how to navigate through that forest. But racism was very real and active. I suppose that situation was an obstacle to be regarded as a stepping-stone that would lead to my divine destination.

Six months later, in July 1971, I decided I could no longer spend time in a position that did not bring me peace and serenity to perform at my best. I could no longer find satisfaction in my labor. I resigned and entered graduate school in August of 1971 at my alma mater, Tennessee State University, to earn a master's degree in guidance and counseling. I wanted to continue my studies in mathematics, but at that time, Tennessee State offered a master's degree only in secondary education with a concentration in mathematics. And I would have to take undergrad courses in the secondary education curriculum before I could start the master's program. I have great respect for educators, but teaching was not my aspiration.

At the time, I had no idea how I was going to pay my tuition. The little money I made while working was spent on clothes to wear to work and help out with the household finances. I applied for financial assistance through the university's Financial Aid Office. When I interviewed with the director of Financial Aid, Homer Wheaton, and he learned that I was the sister-in-law to Professor Betty Van Buren in the Speech and Drama Department at the university, he hired me to work part-time in the office as a financial aid assistant, in addition to giving me financial aid to pay for my tuition and fees. That was a new beginning toward achieving the American dream and finding satisfaction in my work. I was still struggling with the idea of how and where I would be able to apply the rigorous study of mathematics that I had completed. I wasn't even sure how and where I was going to use a degree in guidance and counseling. After studying the exact sciences for four years, studying the experimental sciences was a major transition. Right after I started the master's program, I discovered that I was pregnant. Instead of being a full-time student, my status changed to part-time. My son, Jermayne, was born on May 8, 1972. I was halfway through the degree program when my marriage started to unravel. I completed my master's degree in August of 1974, and in December of 1974, I received my divorce decree that ended my marriage.

Becoming a single parent was not part of my future plans. My dream was to honor the vows that I made the day Williams and I became one. However, debris entered the relationship that caused us to become ineffective individuals to keep the vows we made. I almost lost sight of hope. After I threw off the extra baggage that caused me to take my eyes off the sparrow, I was able to move forward. Faith gave me the wisdom to see when I had become blind. Navigating life was difficult in a world that was so broken. But I was grateful that my faith in the Word was still in my heart to lead and guide me even when I became disorientated. Once my mind was fixed on how I had been raised to trust God, my mind was refocused to be able to see a new path forward. I let go of the life that caused me to doubt my faith. I had to reopen my mind and heart to the faith that I knew assured me that I would not be alone as I searched for a new beginning. Divorce is a cruel and overwhelming experience.

Aside from the civil unrest in our society, civil unrest came through my front door without knocking and upset my social order. I felt hard-pressed on every side, but I was not crushed or struck down. My broken relationship with my husband created a change in my life. But I refused to allow that change to damage my future. I was grateful that my parents raised me in a Christian home that helped me to keep my roots deep in faith so that no matter what happened in my life, I would be able to survive and overcome. I was not going to let my circumstances change my faith, and I did not want to harbor any resentment toward my estranged husband. I was not going to allow the circumstances of my life to affect my state of mind. I had to remind myself that I am a survivor. But living in a world with double standards for women and systemic racism still lingering in our society, I was somewhat unsure of my ability to assume leadership of my family as a single parent.

I reflected on women like Sojourner Truth, a forceful and passionate advocate who was empowered by her religious faith, who used her quick wit and fearless tongue to fight for human rights; Harriet Tubman, responsible for rescuing former slaves from the South and escorting them to freedom via the underground railroad; and Rosa Parks, for her simple act of bravery by refusing to give up her bus seat, just to mention a few women who gave way to a number of improvements in the lives of ordinary Black Americans. How could I not have the courage and strength to think that I could make a difference in some capacity?

In August 1977, circumstances out of my control led me back to Birmingham—the city that I so desperately wanted to leave when I graduated from high school in 1965. I was definitely not excited about the return but economic circumstances left me with no other choice at that time. After I earned my master's degree, I left my position in the Financial Aid Office to work with the Special Services Program as a math specialist at the university. The position was funded by a special federal grant for a period of three years to work with first-year students who were enrolled in remedial math classes at the university. Unfortunately, at the end of the three-year period, my position in the Financial Aid Office was no longer available, and opportunities outside of the university setting were not working in my favor. Once again, I felt that hope for justice and equality was not on my side. I felt like I was going through a Job or Naomi experience.

Returning home as an adult mother with my young son to live with my parents again gave me feelings of both apprehension and hope. Some of my apprehension stemmed from not wanting the pain, hurt, suffering, sorrow, and disappointments that occurred in the 1960s to resurface to my conscious mind. I was apprehensive about employment opportunities. A lot of changes had taken place in Birmingham, but as a whole, the White and Black communities were much the same—with the exception of the area called Bush Hills near Birmingham Southern College, the Graymont area near the Legion Field stadium, and the south side of Birmingham where the University of Alabama Birmingham (UAB) was growing by leaps and bounds. Before I left for college in 1965, the Bush Hills area was a White community. Upon returning to Birmingham, the area was almost all Black, and the remaining Whites were selling their homes and leaving the area like they had been struck by lightning. The same was true with the Graymont area. However, on the south side in and around the University of Alabama Birmingham (UAB) campus, the Black community had been whipped out and converted into the Medical Center of the South.

Fourteen years had passed since the unforgettable day when the most heinous and vicious crime was committed on the House of Worship that took the lives of four innocent girls. The justice department still had not brought anyone to trial. In spite of accumulated evidence that had been found against the named suspects that I mentioned earlier, Robert "Dynamite Bob" Chambliss, Bobby Frank Cherry, Herman Frank Cash, and Thomas E. Blanton Jr., the FBI director J. Edgar Hoover stopped the investigation and ordered the case closed in 1968. Hope for justice had been delayed, but hopefully not denied!

Thanks to a young man named Bill Baxley, who was elected attorney general for Alabama in 1971, the church bombing case was reopened; and he began his own investigation to bring the perpetrators to trial. Attorney General Baxley reported that he was in a position to do what he was sworn to do, solve the Sixteenth Street Baptist Church bombing case. Although files had been destroyed, little physical evidence remained, many of the potential witnesses had died, and many others had long left Alabama, Baxley's relentless investigation uncovered evidence that would convict the main individual responsible for bombing the church. In spite of the danger and threats to his life from the Ku Klux Klan, Baxley got a conviction of murder for Robert "Dynamite Bob" Chambliss in 1977. He was sentenced to several terms of life in prison but proclaimed his innocence until he died in 1985. The victory of Chambliss's conviction lifted most of the cloud of darkness, fear, sorrow, and shame from the city. The victory also took away some of my apprehension to return to Birmingham that year. I am sure the victory eased the hearts and the minds of the parents of the four girls and the Black community. But the cloud of darkness for civil rights would not be completely lifted until the other individuals identified in the investigation were convicted for their role in the bombing.

Twenty-four years later, a team of state and federal attorneys broke the seal on evidence that had been buried in FBI wiretaps that had been ordered sealed by the former director J. Edgar Hoover and other evidence that had remained behind the sealed lips of relatives too scared to talk against Thomas E. Blanton Jr. and Bobby Frank Cherry. The new evidence gave the US attorney Doug Jones the opportunity to take a case that took thirty-eight years to bring to trial. A Birmingham jury of eight Whites and four Blacks convicted Thomas E. Blanton Jr. of murder in May of 2001 for his role in the church bombing. He was sentenced to four terms of life in prison. Bobby Frank Cherry was indicted but did not stand trial with Blanton because Judge Garrett ruled him mentally incompetent. Later, Cherry was found mentally competent to stand trial and was convicted of murder in 2002 for his role in the church bombing. During his prison sentence, Cherry proclaimed to be a victim of a malicious false campaign against him until his death in 2004. Herman Cash, the fourth suspect identified by the FBI as a co-conspirator who maintained his innocence, died in 1994, without being charged.

Finally, my hope for justice had been resolved. From time to time when the memory of the unforgettable day that shamed the nation resurfaced, I would reflect on my faith and remember that I was promised peace if I believed. But there were times when I would become weary while struggling to keep the memory of the unforgettable day suppressed. There were times when quieting my mind was downright impossible. I took comfort in reflecting on what my mother and grandmother used to tell me that a higher power was always fighting for me and working on my behalf. *The Lord will fight for you. You need only to be still* (Exodus 14:14). That same power was also working on behalf of the victim's parents and all the citizens of Birmingham who were seeking justice.

Reflecting back on the season when the unforgettable day occurred, life was full of complications because of the Jim Crow laws. I did not see life through rose-colored lenses. However, there was only one direction for me to travel, and that direction was forward. Realizing that life is a journey, no matter how painful or confusing it may be, I had my faith to lead, guide, and protect each step of my journey. Weathering the storms and evil wills I witnessed, I came to realize that the Spirit of peace had always been living within me. The world could neither take away nor give me peace. I know now that the peace that lives within me is always readily accessible. By finding the peace within myself, I had the power to spread my peace to anyone that I encountered.

Attorney General Bill Baxley and US Attorney Doug Jones, along with their team of investigators, had to have had the Spirit of peace within them to do the right things that allowed justice to prevail. Their humility unified and guided their every decision to bring justice and peace that brought some closure and light to a city that had been clouded with spiritual darkness through the acts of evildoers. The established justice system resolved the murder of the four girls. But, on the other hand, there are two justice systems operating within one nation which affects my hope for complete justice and peace. I believe that in order to change attitudes toward peace, the first step is to look within. From the words of a beloved peace song, "Let there be peace on earth, and let it begin with me." When I think about the words from the Constitution, they don't appear to ensure my domestic tranquility or quiet my fears. Peace is supposed to bring about a state of security within a community and the nation. Peace should also bring freedom from disquieting or oppressive thoughts or emotions. This was the peace I was searching for my heart to feel. However, it was clear that the idea of peacemaking is not always popular, especially among those individuals associated with White supremacy and the KKK. They preferred to fight with violence for what they believed. Since peace would not come without hard work, the glory of any battle is the hope of winning. So the glory of peace-making is that peace will produce two winners.

Chapter 6

<blockquote>

If my people, who are called by my name, shall humble
themselves, and pray, and seek my face, and turn from
their wicked ways; then I will hear from heaven, and
will forgive their sin, and will heal their land.

—2 Chronicles 7:14 (KJV)

</blockquote>

During the Jim Crow era, the Southland was so dark through my eyes that it was difficult to see any goodness in the individuals who created laws that brought suffering to another human being. That period in history was so mind-blogging and painful that searching for deliverance and hoping for unity and healing from the sins of segregation and discrimination seemed far-reaching. The resolution for the murder of the four girls allowed me to see the clouds of darkness gradually being removed from the city of Birmingham. However, the individuals who committed the notorious evil act of bombing the church died without repenting. Their souls left their bodies showing no regrets or contrition.

I realized that I needed to release the negative memories of the past so that I could see the open door of opportunity and begin a new way of thinking without fear, limitations, or restrictions. I am still working on how to release those negative memories. I have to constantly remind myself that all human beings make mistakes. I think it is safe to say from my perspective that racism is a human mistake. When some individuals believe that one race of people is superior to other races and believe that race is the primary determinant of human traits and capabilities, then human beings will continue to be at war with each other. Because racial differences do not produce an inherent superiority of a particular race. I believe that I can safely say that the 1963 bombing of the Sixteenth Street Baptist Church was a human mistake that can never be erased or forgotten. And it was one of the most notorious incidents of racism toward one race of people.

Using the power of my imagination to support my faith, I envisioned positive results as I prayed for healing. I imagined all people living from an awareness of the Creator's presence within their own hearts so that all children everywhere could grow up in a safe and loving environment. My vision for the city of Birmingham was to be united in a common bond of cooperation and goodwill to uphold and support a common goal of bettering the lives of all its citizens. When we learn to see each other through our spiritual eyes, the physical difference will not matter.

I definitely knew that healing my wounds and releasing the painful memories of segregation and discrimination would take time. My feelings of being cheated and excluded from the opportunity to achieve the American dream caused me to have some bitter feelings. But I realized that by holding onto the bitterness and the pain, the wounds from the evil wills of segregation and discrimination would never heal. Although life brought about some bad situations during the Jim Crow era, I have been working to remove the bitterness from my heart and working toward forgiving those who wronged me and the entire race of Black Americans. Holding to the power of faith, I gained the necessary spiritual resources to think positively, act courageously, and move forward. According to the words of Solomon in Ecclesiastes 3:1, "For everything there is a season, and a time for every activity under heaven." This passage of scripture was a reminder to me that God had a plan for me and all people. Although I had faced situations that were unfair and unjust, I believed in due season, the injustice would come to an end at the appointed time.

When I returned to Birmingham in August 1977, the evil wills from the Jim Crow era were still fresh in my mind, although the visible signs were not seen. Realistically, some of the Jim Crow laws were systematically stilled in place. Civil rights for most Black people were still being violated. Most of the public schools were still segregated, as a whole. There were public schools in the city that were both predominately Black and predominately White. However, the predominately White Fairview Elementary School, where the White children in my neighborhood attended during my elementary school years, changed to a middle school where my baby brother Edmond attended and graduated. He later attended Glenn High School in September 1977, which was previously a predominately White school. Because of the White flight from that area, the majority of the students at Glenn High School would soon become predominately Black, studying in the once predominately White school within walking distance from our house. When the Birmingham Board of Education decided to desegregate the public school in 1963, Glenn was not an option for the students in my neighborhood. As a matter of fact, I did not know the school existed until I returned back home in August 1977. The school was a well-kept secret nestled within the Bush Hill and Graymont area that Black people were not allowed to be when I was growing up.

In addition to public schools and the House of Worship, the majority of the neighborhoods were still segregated. While living in Nashville, the environment was similar to Birmingham. I was not totally surprised by the few changes that had been made regarding race relations. In most cases, people were still being judged based on the color of their skin and not by the content of their character, skills, and knowledge. Resistance to civil rights was clearly still a big part of our society.

I was hit head-on with that resistance when I applied for the position of assistant director of Financial Aid at the University of Alabama at Birmingham (UAB) when I was seeking employment. My bachelor's degree in mathematics, master's degree in guidance and counseling, coursework in higher education administration toward my doctoral degree, and prior work experience in financial aid at the university level did not even warrant me an interview. But I did not allow that rejection to make me feel like I was at the end of my rope and hold me back and make me feel inferior. I had faith and believed that the door was going to open for me somewhere. I realized that Birmingham was still implementing the evil wills of discrimination and had not yet reached the recuperation stage.

Even though there were Black Americans in some prominent positions within the city of Birmingham as tokenism, barriers still existed. I had been away from Birmingham for eleven years and did not have any connections within the workforce. As the old cliché says, "It's not what you know but who you know." I mentioned earlier that life is like a camera. So I took that negative experience and kept moving forward and took another shot somewhere else. Even though I was not in control of that job situation, I was not going to be reduced by it. I was just passing through a storm moving toward a brighter light. The March on Washington for equality and justice was not finished but getting close. My faith gave me hope that healing and deliverance were not remote ideas. I was willing to wait patiently for victory to come and not be derailed by that setback. I refused to allow the job situation to make me doubt myself. I had been in that position before when I lived in Nashville. I knew what it meant to have faith and not lose hope. I should have been angry, but my inner spirit would not allow me to be angry, because being angry would cause me to dwell on the negative and keep my eyes from seeing the future opportunities that were before me. It took a whole lot of faith to believe that every day provides fresh opportunities to experience new vistas. The realization that finally confronted me was the fact that I was living in a society that requires the right connections to get hired for most jobs were the prerequisites. No one at UAB knew who I was, and I did not know anyone who knew anyone connected with the university. Once again for me, character, knowledge, and previous work skills were not enough. That situation made me realize that moving beyond our history of racial discrimination in all places was going to take more time. Even though the March on Washington for jobs and equal housing in 1963 took place to remove these barriers, the barriers were still in place. I also realized that the laws created to make us feel incapable of loving one another unless the individual looked like ourselves were still playing a big role in society. But underneath our skin color, the skeleton framework that supports the soft tissues and internal organs of our bodies, we are all the same. That's a simple fact. That is why the big question always kept me wondering why one race of people could think they were superior to another! I also kept wondering if the evil will of racism in society could ever be removed. Racism has been a disastrous evil for hundreds of years that functioned like a serious disease that caused a high rate of mortality in society. From a Christian's point of view, recuperating from a disease as serious as racism, love, patience, courage, and forgiveness are the only cures. Legendary music artist Dionne Warwick's lyrics say, "What the world needs now is love, sweet love. It's the only thing that there's just too little of."

From the principles of Christianity, love is the first dose of medicine society needs to start the healing process from the disease of racism. Scripture tells me that love is the essential reason the world and humanity were created. Love is the most repeated theme throughout the Bible because love is best expressed toward something or someone else. We are all an expression of love, and for that reason, we should love each other. Love is the ultimate expression of our Creator's loyalty, purity, and mercy extended to us to be reflected in our relationships toward each other.

I believe that love is the most powerful force in the universe that is priceless and cannot be bought at any cost. It is freely given. Scripture tells us that there are three things that will last forever—faith, hope, and love—and the greatest of the three is love (1 Corinthians 13:13). Love harmonizes and heals. Imagine a world full of people exploding with love and compassion for one another. Then there would be no room for discrimination and segregation. As human beings, we may have feelings of dislike for a person or group because of race, but we are commanded to love in spite of feelings. We were created to be channels of love and grace. But the world has been filled with so much evil debris that we have failed to be effective channels of love. Because love is the only vehicle that can connect us together in perfect unity.

I considered myself a spiritually intelligent being, blessed with intelligence greater than just my mental IQ. Having that deeper knowledge guided me through those situations in my life when I was met with doubt and uncertainty. My spiritual intelligence had grown to an awareness that when I was faced with challenging circumstances, I was able to move forward with some sense of certainty. My spiritual intelligence would step in and reveal itself as intuition and reminded me that all fruits ripen in their own time. When doubt and uncertainty tried to take a stronghold, I relied on the gift of patience to guide me through and just wait. I have been waiting and hoping to live in a society where the American dream will be like ripe fruit for all Americans to enjoy. Patience played a major role in helping me reclaim my hope.

I believe that patience is the second dose of medicine needed in the process of healing racism from the hearts. Patience is a virtue that most of us need. In truth, patience is another gift from God that belongs to all of us who accept it. For as far back as I can remember, I have struggled with the patience process. I knew that I needed to learn how to be patient, as well as learn how to have a more relaxed attitude toward life. I realized that in order to heal, the mistake of racism would definitely require patience. Patience requires love and understanding for those who made me feel like I didn't measure up to their expectations. Just as it takes patience to plant a tree, to wait for it to send down roots, to take on substance, to grow from a small shoot into maturity; it takes patience to wait for the mistake of racism to heal. I had to remind myself every day that it would take patience to wait for the wounds of segregation and discrimination to heal. I really needed patience and faith to wait for the laws to improve for the good of all mankind. But it was difficult for me to wait for the good to manifest when I felt that I had been deprived long enough. Fear had a way of trying to step in when change was not coming as quickly as I would like. However, I refused to give up on the hope for healing.

According to biblical scholars, Solomon was said to be the wisest man who ever lived. He left us a legacy of written wisdom in three volumes—Proverbs, Ecclesiastes, and Song of Songs. Solomon wrote these three volumes under the inspiration of the Holy Spirit. Within these three books, Solomon gives practical insights and guidelines for living a fulfilled life. In Proverbs 4:23, Solomon tells us to guard our hearts above all else, making sure we concentrate on those desires that will keep us on the right path. My parents gave us strategies for effective living. They always reminded us to make sure that the desires we had in our hearts would lead us in the right direction and not be fooled by flattery. Patience was a key word around our house and probably in most Black American households before and during the Civil Rights Movement times. My parents had to constantly remind me to be patient and keep my mind fixed on my future goal.

I am reminded that Scripture tells us that the hearts of mankind have been filled with evil since Adam and Eve disobeyed God in the garden of Eden. Even after the floodwaters had receded from the earth and Noah and his family were given the signs to come out of the boat and repopulate the earth, the hearts of mankind have been filled with evil wills. With that said, the evil that springs out of our hearts creates the issues that we experience in life. I imagine that's why so much evil was in the atmosphere during the Civil Rights Movement. And the mistake of racism filled our society with the evil wills of segregation and discrimination. This is why I said that patience is the dose of medicine that our hearts need to move beyond those evil wills. Patience is primarily an attitude of the heart toward others. For me, I needed discipline to develop patience. In the process of developing my patience, I learned how to focus my heart on loving all mankind and learn to think of others in an understanding way. Through love and patience, I believed that the mistake of racism could change in due time. But as long as racial stratification continued to occur in employment, housing, education, lending, and government, our society would continue to remain in the recuperation stage far from healing.

When I returned home, fourteen years had passed since I participated in the Children's Crusade. And discrimination and segregation still permeated all aspects of life in Birmingham caused me to reflect back on April 3, 1968, and the dreams of Dr. King when he delivered his final speech in Memphis, Tennessee, when he said, "We, as a people, would get to the Promised Land." That was a prophetic statement made by Dr. King. Just like Moses, Dr. King went to the mountaintop and saw the Promised Land. Just like Moses, Dr. King didn't get to the Promised Land. But as a people, can we truthfully say that the dream has been fulfilled? The big question that is still in my mind is "Have we reached the Promised Land, or are we still wandering in the wilderness?" Questions still remain. Through my eyes, we were still wandering in the wilderness.

History reminds me that Black Americans were a part of this nation before the Pilgrim Fathers landed at Plymouth in 1620, which means that Black Americans helped produce the wealth of this nation. And yet a select group of people in this nation was not willing to share the wealth and power with the people who helped to make America wealthy. Just like Pharaoh used the Hebrews to help build the great cities of Egypt and kept refusing to let them go free. When I searched to get the answer to my "why" questions, I found more questions than answers. Yet even as I struggled with my "why" questions, I held onto hope that someday there would be answers.

I perceived the mistake of racism as spiritual sickness because we live in a sin-sick world. Racism can also be perceived from my perspective as a plague of spiritual darkness that covers the eyes of those whose hearts are filled with hatred, deceit, and privilege. When a small group of selfish individuals clips the wings of the American eagle to feather their nests that excluded other individuals because of race or the color of their skin, the hope for healing continues to be an unfulfilled dream, and America remains blind to the pains of racism. Although no one can make you feel inferior without your consent, the plague of racism that permeates our society is a negative that mankind needs to develop into a positive. Racism will continue to be a serious problem in our nation as long as that small group of selfish Americans believes that they do not have a blind spot about the persistent and widespread impact of racial discrimination.

The hope of healing the plague of this spiritual darkness will require mankind to release old thoughts and beliefs and change old patterns and habits. I realized that it is easy to say and think these words but extremely difficult to put into action. As human beings, we tend to want to hold on to thoughts and beliefs that make us comfortable. For far too many years, Black Americans were not acknowledged as human beings. It sickens me to reflect on the times when we were referenced as their property and used scripture to justify their actions. Yet I am grateful that my ancestors used their inner strength and the power of their being to tear down the walls of slavery and break through the barriers that held them in bondage. Although their bodies had been freed from bondage, there were obstacles that tried to keep their minds from believing it. Faith has a way of intervening and giving you the ability to use your mind and spirit to navigate through the obstacles and believe that you have the power to accomplish anything you set out to do. The Civil Rights Movement in the sixties laid the foundation to open the door to the Promised Land, but most of the accomplishments made by Black Americans seemed meaningless because the majority of Black Americans had not prospered to a significant level. I believed that our Creator meant for each of us to prosper and be blessed in every way. All I wanted was my portion of the sufficient bounty, and I refused to let anyone or anything stop or delay my prosperity.

At the end of August 1977, the door of opportunity opened for me to use my gift of counseling as an outreach counselor at Miles College with the Talent Search Program, a grant funded by the federal government through the Department of Education. I was responsible for reaching out to high school seniors at selected Birmingham City schools who were classified as at-risk students. The Talent Search Program was an extension to the regular counseling services offered to the students at the individual schools. The position did not offer the same monetary rewards as the position of the assistant director of Financial Aid at UAB. But I kept an open mind because success is not measured by monetary rewards. My end goal was about helping at-risk students to have a chance for a better future. I felt blessed to have employment again. And I kept my courage and remained confident in my hope for healing.

To maintain mental and moral strength, again from my perspective, courage is the third dose of medicine needed in the process of healing racism from our hearts. I needed a big dose of courage to maintain my mental and moral strength to continue doing what's morally right. I believe that dismantling racism from our society would definitely require courage on everyone's behalf. It takes strength to be inspired with good courage and act with a firmness of mind and goodwill to face up to the disease of racism. The small group of individuals who continue to believe and convince themselves that one race of people is superior or better than other races are fooling themselves and refusing to acknowledge the truth. It takes courage to change old beliefs and habits and make way for new beginnings for fear of losing who we think we are. But courage helps you overcome feelings of fear. If you think of courage only as a connection with heroism, you fail to understand what true courage means. Not to take away the heroism of the Freedom Riders during the 1960s Civil Rights Movement and the marchers who put their lives on the front line to bring about change; courage is a built-in quality or spirit within everyone that enables you to face difficult circumstances without fear, and not the exclusive property of the physically strong. I am so glad that the Freedom Riders were supplied with both love and patience, along with faith and courage to face the evil wills before them. Because of their courage, some doors opened to Black Americans so that the idea of justice, tranquility, common defense, general welfare, and secured blessings of liberty could be a reality and not just a dream. The Freedom Riders of the 1960s had courage and faith that bridged the chasm of fear that they needed to believe in the best outcome from the worst situations. It took courage and determination for Rosa Parks to refuse to surrender her seat on the bus in Montgomery, Alabama, in 1955. Her courage and grace, along with other unsung heroes whose names are absent from the history books, helped to bring about some change. I like to think of myself as one of the unsung heroes for the role I played in the Children's Crusade March. But I am wise enough to know that my name will be absent from the history books of the future. However, the names of my four friends have already made their mark in history.

I am glad that Dr. King was anointed with the courage to stand up for peace and justice for all mankind. He proclaimed that one day we would all be free when Black Americans would no longer be prisoners in the land of the free. And when White Americans will no longer be blinded by the evil wills of segregation and discrimination. Dr. King's courage and strength enabled him to get the attention of the nation to see how Black Americans in the Southland were being dehumanized by the sinful mistake of racism. He believed in whatever was noble, righteous, and just for all mankind. From that message, I was trying to imagine a world of people with the spirit of nobility, righteousness, and justice for all. When I reflect back on history, the Civil War was the deadliest military conflict in American history. It was sinful that so many lives were lost just to keep Black Americans as slaves in the Southern states. Thank God, the Northern states were victorious and preserved the United States as one nation and ended the institution of slavery. The Civil War was not a noble or righteous act, because the end of slavery created racism that our nation continues to wrestle with today.

From my perspective, I believe that the process of dismantling racism in our society will take indomitable strength and courage on the part of each and every American to learn to live with each other in perfect peace and love. That is why I believe that courage dwells within all of us at all times. It gives us the strength to be the peaceful and loving human beings that we were created to be. The courage that dwells within me keeps me from harboring negative thoughts and actions. I often wondered why so much evil had been plotted against Black Americans. It was courage that gave me the strength to move forward even in the face of trials. My strong belief system in faith gives me the ability to approach life experiences with boldness even when there were times when it was difficult to make sense of the intangible obstacles and the limitations I faced at every turn. I had to keep the faith and believe that my future plans for reclaiming my hope would prevail *and* not grow weary while the healing takes place.

I realized that I was living in a mixed-up and tarnished world that was cursed by Adam and Eve. Adam and Eve knew what life was like before the curse. They could remember the world the way our Creator intended it to be—free of unnecessary death, hardship, and pain (Genesis 3:16–17). Before the curse, no one questioned God's creative power or his plan for human relationships. Now we live in a good world, full of individuals gone wrong. Segregation, discrimination, and racism did not exist before the curse. The world today does not measure up to God's original design plan for the world. The world today is so broken and filled with an endless supply of evil wills all around us. Yet, in spite of the cloudy memory of what the world should have been like, the past and its consequences cast a shadow on the promise of something better. That is why I believe we have to acknowledge the sins of the past and not turn a blind eye to our history and be responsible for making things right. However, to me, there seems to be a constant struggle in the world because humanity seems to keep doing the things that we know should not be done. We know racism is wrong as well as an evil mistake, yet it continues to spread throughout our society, like wildfire. So the question remains, *How do we put out the fire?* My faith has given me the courage to keep walking through the fire, while our society keeps working toward removing the evil wills of racism and restoring the people of this world to measure up to the original design plan.

Even after the 1960s Civil Rights Movements, America was still refusing to face that racism in our society continued to be a major issue. The visible barriers were no longer staring us in the face, but more modern indirect forms of expression of racism have taken over the visible barriers. Racism undermines the ideals of our Constitution that every American should have equal rights under the law; but thanks to reformers like Harriet Tubman, Frederick Douglass, and Martin Luther King, Jr., who envisioned America as an inclusive nation strengthened by diversity and free of discrimination, the idea of equality will gradually allow us to transform our nation to become more like God's original design plan. However, as long as the powerful and the privileged continue to stir prejudice to further their ends, the mistake of racism will continue to plague our society. But I will continue to hold to the truth that all men are created equal and endowed by the Creator with certain unalienable *rights*—life, liberty, and the pursuit of happiness.

I thought the 1963 demonstrations in Birmingham made a significant impact and laid the foundation to shape the future for the city and the nation toward equality and justice for all citizens. However, sharing of power between Black and White Americans in the city government of Birmingham had only made little gains in the political realm. Not until 1967, Attorney Arthur Shores, the first Black American, was appointed to fill a vacated seat on the Birmingham City Council. The positive outcome of that appointment was his reelection to serve a full term in 1968. But that was a mere tokenism of change in the political realm. Really! Nashville, during that time, had a much better representation of Black Americans serving in city politics *but* not a significant number to wow about. So *why does the number matter to me?* From the mind of a mathematics major, a number is a mathematical object used to count, measure, label, and sometimes restrict. I have been counted, measured, labeled, and restricted since the day I was born. I understand the power of a number as a person who has not always been treated in a friendly way. The power of a number goes back to the beginning when God created the earth and all his creatures and mankind. A number determines where you can live and the quality of how you live.

The demographics of the city began to change when the elite and middle-class White Americans moved to the suburbs surrounding the city. With the White flight, the composition of the inner city was mostly of Black Americans. The demographics of the inner city, comprising mostly Black Americans, led to the election of the second Black member, Dr. Richard Arrington Jr., a biology professor at Miles College, to the Birmingham City Council in 1971. Birmingham was not what it used to be and was far from being perfect. The city still had a long way to go to honor the promises it held for Black Americans' civil rights. The continued problem of police brutality even after hiring a few Black American officers in the late 1960s kept the wounds of distrust between Black Americans and White Americans from completely healing.

It was very clear to me that the process of change and growth can be both difficult and fearful. Returning to a place that I thought of as shameful and full of evil and hatred was difficult but not as fearful as I felt in the past. But it was difficult for me to reunite to worship at Sixteenth Street Baptist Church. When I attended worship service after my return home, I could not focus on the worship service. Each time I attended, I felt like I was reliving the unforgettable day all over again. My mother and brother Edmond were still members of the church. My mother wanted me to reunite, but I was having trouble moving beyond the memory of that day fourteen years later. My mother was not at the church when the bomb exploded, so she did not have the same memory of that day that I suppressed in my subconscious for years, only to have to resurface each time I entered the sanctuary. I did not really realize the impact of that day until I returned and tried to gain a sense of normality. So I joined Sardis Baptist Church, where I became an active member. Changing my membership to a different church helped to suppress the memory of that unforgettable day each time I entered the sanctuary at Sixteenth Street Baptist. It has been utterly impossible for me to lose the remembrance of that day the bomb exploded, yet I am grateful that I survived. I only wish that my four friends could have survived as well.

As I settled into living life in Birmingham as an adult, I had to figure out if I wanted to reignite myself as a civil rights activist or move in a different direction. I also had to make decisions related to my personal life. For two years after I moved back home, my son and I lived with my parents and my baby brother Edmond. My income level at that time did not allow me to live the lifestyle I had been accustomed to. During that period, I saved enough money for a down payment on a house in the Bush Hills area, five blocks from my parents' home where I grew up. Sad to say that it took fourteen years for Black Americans to live in that location. And that's only because of the White flight to the suburbs. They left their old crumbs in the city and moved on to something bigger, better, and new. Clearly, income disparity was a major issue still looming in the economic system. However, I was truly grateful as a single Black woman to be able to purchase my first home in the spring of 1979. The house that I purchased was similar to my parents' house with only a few-square-footage difference. My house had a dining room and my parents' house did not. And they purchased their home when it was new back in 1946. The one I purchased was over thirty years old. But it had been well-kept and updated when needed. The purchase of the house gave me back my independence. Thank God! No matter how old you are, living under your parents' roof takes away your independence.

There were no pressing civil rights issues at the forefront, other than Black Americans taking a more prominent role in the political spectrum. Birmingham's city government was on an upward swing toward electing more Black Americans to city council positions. The year 1979 was a pivotal year in the political history for Birmingham and the state of Alabama when Dr. Richard Arrington Jr. became the first Black American elected to hold the office of mayor. That was a landmark in the city's political history. During the campaign period, I played an active role as a volunteer at the campaign office to help get Dr. Arrington elected. That was my first experience of community service in the political realm. I had the opportunity to see firsthand how political campaigns worked at the local level. Politics had never been a particular interest to me in the past, because from my perspective, politics is about power and control. And from what I had witnessed from the past years, Black Americans had little to no political power and no voice where it mattered. From that standpoint, I never had the need to establish any political values. However, I always exercised my right to vote when I became legally eligible to register when I lived in Nashville, Tennessee. My political views resonate somewhat with the political scientist Harold Lasswell, who defines politics as "who gets what, when, and how." I also viewed politics as another means for certain people to have power and control that take advantage and exploit political relationships to deal with people in an opportunistic, manipulative, or devious way. In my view, the political system was designed to keep Black Americans in their place and limit them to the prosperity of this earth.

I had the opportunity as a campaign worker to see from the inside that politics favored the privileged class and the powerful wealthy people. But Dr. Arrington ran a grassroots campaign that engaged ordinary people like me to help get the people in the Black communities registered to vote. Birmingham at that time had more registered White voters than Black voters, but Dr. Arrington was able to get complete support from the Black community and picked up the necessary White votes to win the election. That political landmark laid the foundation for more growth and change that began the process of the removal of some of the inequalities among the people in the city of Birmingham. However, courage was the motivating factor that led the people in the city of Birmingham to move beyond racial barriers and elected the right individual that would help to lift the cloud of darkness from the city and widen the door to a new beginning. That political landmark was a path toward upward mobility for Black Americans to achieve some economic power within the city. Although White Americans continued their move to the suburbs surrounding the city, the middle-class Black American began to show growth, but the economic gap between Black and White Americans was still too wide. The racial divide would ultimately never mend, as long as White Americans continued to run away from the mistakes of racism, instead of coming together.

That point of view brought me to the foremost needed dose of medicine to totally correct and dismantle the mistake of racism and pardon the sins of the past—forgiveness. If racism could be written in the sands and the waves of the ocean gently wash away the word, then Birmingham, the entire Southland, and our nation could experience release, peace, and justice for all mankind. The continued existence of racism does not serve the best interest of our nation. But the hearts of most Americans continued to be hardened and turned a deaf ear to the matter.

I considered myself to be flexible and forward-thinking, with awareness as to who I am and why I am here. For that reason, I had to find a way to stop reliving the memory of the unforgettable day when the bomb exploded at the church as well as the painful memories of the Jim Crow era. I did not want to continue dwelling on hopelessness. My hope for healing, releasing, and letting go of the past motivated me to tell my story. I needed to cast aside what was weighing me down so that my mind could feel free, refreshed, and rejuvenated. As I released what I no longer needed to suppress in my subconscious, a new sense of understanding about this life journey was unleashed in me. At the same time, my painful memories from the past which I was holding onto left me wondering if my life's journey was going to get me where I wanted to be in the future. I needed to release all the doubts, questions, and fears, and cling to the hopes that would emerge out of the past experiences that had shaped my life so far.

Malcome X quoted, "A man who stands for nothing will fall for anything." Robert Dynamite Bob Chambliss, Thomas E. Blanton, and Bobby Frank Cherry—all convicted of the murder of the four girls Addie, Carol, Cynthia, and Denise, who were killed in the church bombing—stood for nothing! They had succumbed to hatred and bigotry promoted by the hate group called the KKK. Chambliss, Blanton, and Cherry, along with all the Klan members, had to be stonyhearted individuals in order to carry out all the heinous and vicious crimes committed by the organization. Chambliss and Cherry did not have the decency to ask for forgiveness. They died proclaiming that they were innocent and had been framed for the crime. Based on Alabama laws, Blanton would have been eligible for parole on April 1, 2016. Thank God! Justice took a stand on August 3, 2016, when the Alabama Board of Pardons and Paroles denied his early release after serving only fifteen years of four life sentences. He never showed any remorse or asked for forgiveness. Yet he continued to claim his innocence until death. Their spiritual philosophy must have been filled with hate, intolerance, and anger. The spirit of love is the guiding force that inspires individuals to do what is right and good. I believe that the seeds that helped to create and preserve discrimination and segregation in our society should have a moral responsibility to want to correct the mistake of racism. I view racism as morally wrong and deadly. I know that forgiving the mistake of racism would be the essential component of the healing process for me. However, the memories of the past are rooted so deep in my soul that the forgiving process was a choice that I needed to make to restore my soul and release the pain and hurt in my heart.

I wanted to believe that the world could one day function like the initial design plan that God put in place at the beginning of creation.

Moving forward, I kept dreaming of a world where Americans could think of inclusion instead of exclusion. That would be a major crossroad toward diversity. I know that no one can be forced to forgive, because forgiveness is a choice and a gift to both give and receive. So I chose to forgive in order to release the painful situations that I experienced during the Children's Crusade March and when the church was bombed. But it does not mean that I condone what happened—I simply choose to let go. Those experiences have only as much power over me as I give them. I could let the memories of the Jim Crow era hold me back or I could move beyond that mistake. I chose not to carry the weight of that emotional pain forever and to be free from resentment, anger, and hurt. Just like the ocean waves crash and roll over the beach in a repetitive cadence, rising and falling, rolling in and out, regardless of the weather, season, or changes on the shore, I have learned how to release and forgive and to try to imagine a world of people drawing inspiration from the continuous movement of the ocean waves to release and forgive. I believe that once Americans take notice of the awful mistake of racism and acknowledge the problem, the change process for forgiveness can begin. And they will be free from hate and bigotry.

I know that change is difficult, but I had to embrace change again when my son Jermayne and I relocated to Atlanta, Georgia, in August 1987. My employment contract had come to an end at Miles College. My employment career at Miles began in August 1977. I was an outreach counselor and was later promoted to the position of the director of Admissions and Records and then later to become the director of Institutional Research, and finally, as an assistant director in the Student Financial Aid Office, which was a demotion. The Institutional Research position was very political which had me at the beck and call of the president overseeing the endowment program for the college. I was naïve about how to play the political game to stay at that level, so I was repositioned to the Office of Student Financial Aid until my contract ended in June 1986. At first, I felt humiliated and a sense of failure because I had been in that kind of circumstance before. Here again, faith stepped in to help me restore hope and trust that God had other plans for my future. So I used that unemployment time to earn my teaching credentials at the University of Alabama at Birmingham (UAB) to teach mathematics at the high school level. With that new situation in my life, I felt like I was back in the womb of darkness. I had to remind myself of the words from my mother to stay hopeful because out of the darkness, there will be light at the end of the tunnel. Now once again I was giving up my roots, the place where I was born and raised. The place where I once was ashamed to call home. After completing the requirements to receive my Alabama Teacher's Certificate, the city of Birmingham had a freeze on hiring teachers because of budget constraints. My father, who passed away in March 1985, was always there for me whenever I had to weather a financial storm; but this time around, I had to trust and believe that my faith would help me weather the storm and get me through. Although Birmingham had a freeze on hiring, my sister informed me that all the school systems in Atlanta, Georgia, had a shortage of mathematics teachers. Submitting my application to the top three school systems—Atlanta, Fulton, and Dekalb—was my hope for a way out of the womb of darkness. The Dekalb County School System was the first to acknowledge my application and offered me a contract the same day that I was interviewed. During that temporary period in the womb of darkness, I was being fed, nurtured, and gaining new strength that lightened my load and helped to heal my pain so that my heart would be open for the new life. At that same time, my hope for racial healing for the city of Birmingham continued to move in a direction that would foster inclusiveness and forgiveness. When I reflect on the past and think about how I overcame the insurmountable obstacles of the Jim Crow laws, I was somewhat optimistic about the future for Black Americans. However, I think that much more change is needed to advance the economic mainstream and work toward an upward mobility in the political realm for Black Americans—because the evil wills of systemic racism were still quietly looming in the air.

I realize and understood that healing the mistake of racism would not be easy, because old habits die hard, but the idea of dismantling the mistake of racism has to stay on the front burner so that White Americans will not be let off the hook and try to turn back the hard-fought gains of the Civil Rights Movement for equality and justice under the law for all Americans. I believe that we need to constantly remind ourselves of the achievements made during the movement and continue the stride to help all Black Americans and other people of color achieve the American dream that promotes general welfare and secure blessings of liberty for all. I have witnessed a lot of progress in healing the mistakes of racism, but it has not yet arrived for all Americans. I hold onto hope that one day America will realize that racism is sin—pure and simple, then the process for healing can begin. And the process of stripping away the old habits of hate and bigotry can also begin.

Chapter 7

Together as one body, Christ reconciled both groups
to God by means of his death on the cross and our
hostility toward each other was put to death.

—Ephesians 2:16 (NLT)

*I am reminded that history records many past events that have simi-
larities.* According to Ecclesiastes 1:9, "History merely repeats itself.
Nothing under the sun is truly new." So, from that perspective, the
Civil Rights era had a resemblance to a time in history when the
Gentiles and the Jews kept apart from each other. The Jewish laws
favored the Jews and excluded the Gentiles. Just like the Jim Crow
laws favored White Americans and excluded Black Americans. Just
as the Gentiles resented the Jews, Black Americans resented White
Americans because they felt that they were superior above all other
races. According to Scripture, God sent his Son to earth to destroy
the barriers that people built between themselves and ended the
angry resentment between the Jews and Gentiles. Christ abolished
the whole system of Jewish laws and unified the Jews and Gentiles as
"one new people" and fused them together to become one in Christ.

The Jim Crow era kept White Americans and Black Americans
apart from each other under many circumstances. Christ came to
earth long before the civil rights era to break down the walls of prejudice and injustice. His death on the Cross freed us from our sins.
Yet today many Americans are still following the old evil ways and
desires of the past to preserve racism. As Americans, I believe that if
we seek racial reconciliation as a new way of life, then it would be
possible to ensure a true transition into a diverse society and perhaps

learn how to create harmony amongst each other, just as God desires. Although the civil rights era brought about some notable changes in behavior and racial attitudes, systematic racism continued to be pervasive in American life. The legacy of racism takes us back to two hundred years of brutal slavery and one-hundred-plus years of segregation and discrimination. So *how can the mistake of the legacy of racism be reconciled?* I personally don't have the answer. But I do believe that we can learn how to recognize our racial differences and embrace them so that we can know how our racial identities uniquely contribute to the big picture to create a nation of peace and harmony.

Even at a much younger age, I could clearly see the inequity and discrimination everywhere. That made me feel at times that God must not love Black Americans. I was being faced with spiritual attacks that were trying to rob me of hope. So I had to remind myself that according to God's Word, the idea that God must not love Black Americans couldn't be true. When I would hear my grandmothers, my mother, and the pastors talk about the pie in the sky, I thought I wanted my pie right here on earth because I don't know anyone who has gone to the sky and returned to earth to verify that fact. Scripture tells me about eternal life. However, I could see plenty of pie right here on earth being enjoyed by White Americans. It appeared to me that most White people were privileged—enjoying the pie, the cake, the ice cream, and everything else right here on earth. Why not me? It was so apparent that I was living in a world plagued with racial inequality because of people with "messed-up minds" and evil hearts. Most White Americans appeared to be oblivious to the reality of privileges given to them automatically. And through their eyes, they couldn't see the systemic advantages afforded to them every single day.

From that point of view, I imagine that mending the mistakes of the past and moving toward racial reconciliation would take effort, sacrifice, and a whole lot of love. Reconciliation means to change or to cause a change. That is why I believe that transformation of the hearts and attitudes of the privileged would help the process of racial reconciliation and help mend the painful past mistakes of racial discrimination. I also believe that the reconciliation process begins when we as a people identify with each other and stand in solidarity. I know that's a tall order! Based on the history of racial discrimination in our nation, the mistakes of racism cannot be erased, because that would mean the past three-hundred-plus years did not exist. Even during the past three-hundred-plus years, I believed that there had been some good-hearted White Americans who felt guilty and would genuinely like to see racism ended. So the question is, *How do we end racism?* I believe the simple answer to the question could be *one step at a time.* But through my lens, I do not see any serious steps moving in the direction to end racism. Like the quote from the Twi proverb—"You must eat the elephant one bite at a time." Like the elephant, racism is a big issue all over the world, not just in America.

Attorney General Bill Baxley stood up for justice and got a conviction for Robert "Dynamite Bob" Chambliss for his role in the Sixteenth Street Baptist Church bombing. That was the first opportunity for racial reconciliation to right the wrong that also led to the conviction of the other individuals involved in the bombing. When the citizens in the city of Birmingham stood together to elect the first Black mayor in 1979, that was another small step toward racial reconciliation. During the civil rights campaign, the citizens of the city of Birmingham acknowledged their grievances and did what had to be done to make peace. That was a time when unity was desperately needed to show that as human beings we could agree to come together and avoid open confrontation. Those actions were signs of racial reconciliation.

It seemed clear to me that we are already unified through the breath that flows throughout our bodies that keeps us alive each and every day. This makes me wonder why we continue to deny our unity because we look different, act different, and believe we want different things. As long as we continue to feel that way, I believe that's what makes racial healing a remote idea. I think about all the different trees on planet earth living together to create the mighty forest. The sea creatures living together to create the wealth of the ocean. The wild animals living together in the wonderment of the wild and the creatures in the sky singing together in harmony. And wonder why we as humans find it so difficult to live that way. In reality, we all want the same things: food, shelter, protection, and an opportunity to move freely without fear. I believe that if we respect the power in our differences and stop blaming and judging because of our differences, racial reconciliation can take place.

First and foremost, we are all human beings, which gives us a certain amount of power to not be limited in how we express our humanness. But because of the labels applied to human beings, the boundaries and limits are set, keeping us from crossing and reconciling. Labels limit us and set up expectations that keep us from embracing our differences. When I think about what past generations of Black Americans have had to overcome, I had to remind myself that this life journey does not always move along a straight path. In addition to keeping an open mind about hope for the future. Hoping for a path to achieve racial reconciliation. And recognize how racial inequality personally affects all of us. Hoping that we will not continue to ignore our racial identities but embrace the difference. Then the hope for equality for all mankind, I believe, can be achieved.

My hope and belief for the journey for racial reconciliation in Birmingham, Alabama, and our nation could begin by leaving the comfort and familiarity of our racially isolated worlds and begin engaging across racial lines. God has made it clear to us that we are to be reconciled not only to him but also to each other. My hope is that one day we will be able to look at all people in the world with a new perspective that demands us to take a stand for unity and not take sides. When we harbor racist thoughts and behaviors, we are denying the reality that each of us is created in the image and likeness of God. Scripture tells us that God did not create one race of people to be superior or have power over another. So the question that puzzles my mind is, *How did we get here?*

I would imagine that to find an answer to that question required looking back at the nation's history that has been stained with the ugliness of racial discrimination and prejudice that was justified by some by misrepresenting Scripture to make bigoted behavior and thoughts seem right and just. I feel privileged having been raised by parents who instilled in me the belief that there is some good in everybody in spite of the bigotry that I witnessed. Yet because racism has been embedded in the fabric of our society for such a very long time, the racial wounds are still visible in my mind today. And I'm sure in the minds of other Black Americans from that time who are still living. Events happening today reopens my old wounds that were trying to heal. The racial scars in my mind are very deep. My soul had been wounded, but for years, I pretended not to be hurt. Yet every time I was confronted with the memory of the events that caused the scars, the wounds are reopened. After I finally admitted to myself that the wounds exist and I began to examine and expose them to myself, I learned to love and respect myself more because, at every turn, society was telling me otherwise. So I learned how to wrap my racially scarred wounds in the most potent antiseptic there is—love. Because I am a child of God, and he chose me to survive. Knowing that his strength, wisdom, power, and love are being expressed as me, I have been able to free my mind of some of the debris and wait for hope and restoration to come.

When I reflect back on my roots beyond my parents and grandparents and think about my family line of geniuses who were born into a barren land and built the pyramids in Egypt, charted the stars, and kept time by the sun and planted by the moon, I have no doubt about my ability to survive and thrive in a nation plagued with evil wills. In the cells of my bloodstream are the memories of my ancestors who weathered the voyage, found their way through the forest, and took their case all the way to the Supreme Court. Even though as a Black American living in a society that denies my history, culture, and traditions, I am still able to stand tall in a world where your skin color matters more than your character. As much as some people want to believe otherwise, skin color does matter, because racism still exists in our society. This goes back to my question earlier: *How did we get here?*

When I relocated to Atlanta, Georgia, in August 1987, I took on the responsibility to impart the mathematical knowledge that I learned with the students at Cross Keys High School in the Dekalb School System. I was certain that I was ready to greet the task at hand with joy and anticipation. I was excited to have the opportunity to help students apply a positive and open approach to the process of learning mathematics. However, I found myself wondering, *How did I get here?* My initial goal in life was not to become an educator. Yet eighteen years after graduating from undergraduate school with a degree in mathematics, the spirit called me to become *a helper*. Even though my prior work experiences had been in the academic arena at the higher educational level, I was not classified as an educator but as an administrator. I answered the call of life to play my part in the amazing world of educators. That's when I realized again that the color of my skin mattered. I believed that I was hired because I was qualified to take on the task. But I was also hired so that the school system could meet a mandated quota to hire Black Americans and females to fill positions in the area of mathematics and science. The high school where I was assigned had only one other Black American female mathematics teacher and no Black male teachers in the mathematics department. The student body demographic was predominately White with a small percent of bused-in minority-to-majority students and a small percent of international students from Nigeria, Ethiopia, South Africa, both Central and South America, Dominican Republic, Asia, and Mexico. The school at that time was classified as an international school. Students from the International Center were bused in during the last two periods of the school day to learn language arts and mathematics. The language of mathematics is considered universal, so even though the international students had not completely mastered the English language, most of them were able to excel in mathematics. Looking at the big picture, the environment at the school was considered racially diverse. Racial difference did not appear to be a visible issue. However, at the end of the school day, our individual lives took us back to an environment that was racially divided. While progress in our nation has been made in the area of diversity, we are not yet where we should be. As I looked around the community where I lived, I could see many things that indicated more change was needed to improve the racial divide. But I was not going to give up my hope for racial reconciliation. I believe that if we stop and take a look inside ourselves, the fear and anger between the races can be eliminated. Then the path forward to reconcile the mistake of racism can happen.

The apartment complex where I lived when I first moved to Atlanta was racially mixed but racially divided by units. All the tenants in the unit where I lived were all Black Americans. The only time I saw the White tenants in the complex was when they were at the swimming pool area. They would leave anytime someone Black came to the pool area when they were there. Twenty-four years after the Civil Rights Movement, I was having a hard time believing that there were still some White Americans who did not want to be in the company of Black Americans on a social level. It was hard for me to understand this kind of behavior. Even hurtful at times. But faith was the key that helped to sustain me and hold onto hope. I also relied on God's Word to help me understand the madness about skin color. Although skin color is not mentioned in the Bible, it is definitely implied. Interracial mixing took place when God scattered the people among the earth to multiply after the curse in the garden of Eden. This means that offspring produced from interracial mixing have been going on before the slave trade in America. However, man created worldly laws, not heeding the instructions of God, to divide the races and made it unlawful to comingle outside one's own race and culture, causing racism to become an issue in our society. That is why from my perspective, racism is sin—pure and simple.

It was hard for me to imagine how anyone could harbor such sinful thoughts that caused racism to become a systemic problem manifested by personal, cultural, and economic reasons. Some White Americans tried to reduce the problem of racism to individual acts of meanness. The problem goes deeper than just acts of meanness. Racism has been like a forest fire burning in our lives but tackled like small brushfires—the Freedom Riders, the sit-in demonstrations, the protest marches, and the urban riots of the 1960s. Those small brushfires were causes to confront, battle, and overcome. However, the forest is still on fire. Because open conservation and acknowledgment of racial inequality has not been placed on the table to confront, probably because the process of racial reconciliation comes with a cost that most people are not willing to pay. Jesus paid a high price in his pursuit of reconciliation which led to his death on the Cross. John F. Kennedy and Dr. Martin Luther King Jr. were both assassinated for their pursuits of reconciliation. However, I hope that the process of racial reconciliation may or may not require us to experience a physical death like Jesus, Kennedy, King, and other unsung heroes. However, I do believe that we will have to experience the death of cultural idolatry, personal power or group-based power, and ethnocentricity. Those forms of death would be excruciating for some people—the people who appear to be oblivious to the reality of privilege given automatically and invisibly to them every single day. For that reason, racism has continued to spread like a forest fire. My hope was that racial reconciliation could become an ongoing way of life. Because we are all created from the same spiritual substance—every person, every creature, every atom, every cell. That is why I view the idea that skin color being used to keep us separate from one another as just pure evil thinking.

Having to navigate my way through the world of stereotypes regarding Black Americans, I felt the responsibility to prove myself anew each and every day *because* I would never be given the benefit of doubt and there was no margin for error. In spite of the stereotypes regarding Black Americans and the Jim Crow laws, I can remember during the fifties, the sixties, and the seventies, the city of Birmingham had Black doctors, nurses, dentists, lawyers, accountants, Black own restaurants, investment banks, real estate agencies, architectural firms and Black owned radio station that were thriving in the Black business communities. Other professionals like educators and laborers represented the middle class of Black Americans. However, we were definitely not equal from an economic perspective in spite of the small section of downtown Birmingham allocated for Black-owned businesses. And White Americans certainly did not spend their dollars in the Black business community. The window that I was looking through did not show me an America that was great. Nor did I see an America that was honoring the words of the Constitution of the United States of America.

Even though the legacy of the Civil Rights Movement helped, to a small degree, widen the doors to some jobs and housing opportunities, there were still roadblocks in the late eighties for Black Americans in the corporate world and municipal government opportunities. Although affirmative action programs were in place to break down barriers, both visible and invisible; level the playing field; and make sure everyone was given an equal break. However, White Americans were consistently preferred for a job, when buying a house, or when given a bank loan than Black Americans and other minorities who were equally as qualified. This means that the playing field for justice and equality still has yet to be leveled. I understand that old habits are not easily broken and reaching out beyond the race boundaries is a matter of the heart. The heart is the core of an individual. However, the word *heart* has a wide range of applications. Focusing on the will application, the heart is the seat of the will of an individual, which is the source of good or evil qualities or behavior. The Bible characterizes the human heart as full of evil (Genesis 8:21), deceitful and corrupt (Jeremiah 17:9), and in need of transformation through God's grace (Psalm 51:10; Ezekiel 36:26). I injected these references to make the point that an individual's thoughts, intentions, and feelings are motivated and driven by the heart.

Because of the intentions of the heart, I know that ending racism in our country and the world will take a long time. I may not be around when the end comes. But because racism has been such an unpleasant and painful experience for me and other Black Americans, I want it to end quickly. I know that I cannot rush the sun to rise or pay to bring on the full moon. And I know that the process of racial reconciliation was not in my control. And I understand that there's a process to transforming hearts and minds to become instruments of God's love, peace, and justice. This means that all Americans have to be willing to move forward one step at a time to achieve a new way of life. When I think about what past generations of Black Americans, myself, and other minorities have had to overcome to get where we are, I remain hopeful that racial reconciliation can be achieved by better enforcement of existing civil rights laws and implementing new laws that will respect the lives of all citizens in this nation regardless of the color of their skin. My hope and dreams were to be seen as just another human being in spite of the pigmentation of my skin.

Moving from Birmingham to Atlanta and getting assigned to teach at a school that was racially diverse gave me hope that racial reconciliation had a future. Even though the day-to-day environment outside the school building didn't always show that sign. For twenty-three years, I used the classroom as my stage to employ my ability to empower and encourage students to understand, appreciate, and apply life's application to the study of mathematics. I did what I could for the sake of doing it without pursuing recognition or worldly rewards. Knowing that my students, regardless of their race, benefited and harvested from the seeds that I planted was my recognition and reward. I understood that the key to success was not what I was doing but how I felt about what I was doing.

I tried to radiate an energy of love and peace each and every day even during the times when I was met with opposition from some of my students and even some parents who thought because of the color of my skin, I was not qualified to teach them in spite of the fact that I met the requirements to receive my degree in mathematics in addition to meeting the required standards to hold a certificate that certified that I had met the state requirements to be a teacher. Somehow, I was able to access infinite peace within myself to think consciously and react in peaceful ways. I leaned on the divinely inspired peace that dwells inside me to harvest the courage and strength to withstand the attacks against me and held onto hope that racism could eventually be dismantled if we join together to speak and listen to each other in a spirit of openness and trust. That is why I listened to my students with an open heart, their thoughts, opinions, and desires, without judgment to create an environment of trust. Imagine a world where all the people are honestly embracing the past mistakes of racism to live more peacefully and truthfully in the present and in the future. Then the inequalities of the past will no longer dictate the possibilities of the future. Outside of my classroom and school, I envision a society and a world where people of all races are treated equally and everyone has equal access to the opportunities of the riches of this land. I believe that I was successful in shaping the minds of most of my students to respect our differences and transcend their thoughts to a level of kindness toward one another.

From my position as a teacher in a racially diverse school setting, I tried to create an awareness that racial harmony would establish relationships across racial and ethnic lines. I believe that my students knew that I had a Christian heart, not only because I kept my Bible on my desk in plain view when prayer and religion had no place in schools but because of the way that I respected them as individuals. In spite of the "no prayer" rule, I prayed throughout the school day silently to God to guide my every thought and word. Taking prayer out of schools was one of the ways for the evil wills of the powerful to continue to suppress. That is why I continue to identify racism as a sin. And I truly believe that biblical applications would be an effective way to address the racial reckoning issue. There are many issues in the classroom that teachers and students have to deal with, but racism is one of the most controversial issues that people fight every day to defend their views. Racism, whether we want to admit it or not, is a daily battle that is spoken out loud by some and whispered by others. Some of the students in my classroom were from mixed-race families. And I am sure they were directly affected by the issue every day.

The church is definitely affected by the issue. Sunday is still the most segregated day in the world today. I am so glad that there are still some people on the front lines getting wounded and scarred fighting the struggle regarding racial reconciliation. According to Scripture, the harvest is plentiful, but there are only a few reconcilers who are willing to take up the sword of truth and shield of faith and join the front lines to help dismantle racism. *I wonder why.* Are those individuals who claim superiority and privilege too afraid to face the real truth? That is why I choose to categorize racism as an institutionalized system. And it acts like a nasty virus that lies dormant in the body for a long time and flares up under certain particular circumstances. I believe that searching within one's heart, facing the bigotry, and doing something about it are the ways to move toward racial healing. I was fully aware that the system of racism operates twenty-four hours a day, seven days a week, without mercy or letting up. This made me wonder if my hope for healing was just a big dream. Even within my diverse school setting, I could feel the invisible racist practices on a daily basis. I didn't want to believe that a great deal of racism was unconscious and unintended. As a human, I do believe that you are aware of your unconscious behaviors. Because every available strategy was being used to keep racism alive unconsciously. James Baldwin described it this way, "White people wanted to stay blind to the reality that they do not want to know the meaning, or face the shame of what they compelled—out of what they took as the necessity of being White." According to the history that I learned, racism is basically the product of the slave trade or the seizure of power. That is the reason that I believe shallow-hearted individuals believe that power and control belong to the created privileged—the reason visible and invisible signs of racism continue to plague us. It will take strength and resilience on all of us to make a difference toward racial healing. It's a matter of the heart!

I think that the problem with racism, from my perspective, is that it cannot be defined. However, *Webster* defines *racism* as "the poor treatment of or violence against people because of their race" and "the belief that some races of people are better than others." Realistically, however, *Webster* only gives us a description of *racism*. Just like the undefined terms in the study of geometry—points, lines, planes, and space can only be identified, labeled, and described. That is why I describe, label, and identify *racism* as sin—pure and simple. From a biblical perspective, sin is a moral evil, a transgression of, or a rebellion against God's laws, an offense or fault against God, or the act of breaking God's laws. So the moral evil called racism fueled by man is a rebellion against God's laws, the Creator. Therefore, it is clear from my understanding that, until we realize that it is our responsibility to seek direction from God on how to address racism, the brokenness of humanity everywhere will continue to exist.

I have always relied on my faith and spiritual convictions to guide me each and every day while I travel the journey of life. But in September 1998, I was met with a situation that almost knocked me out of the game of life. My only son at the age of twenty-six was murdered by Birmingham police officers. Just when I was beginning to believe that Birmingham was on the road toward reconciling the difficult and painful memories of the past police brutality toward

Black Americans, my son became a victim. The Birmingham Police Department described the situation as a gun battle between my son and the police. However, the autopsy report indicated that no gun residue was found anywhere on my son's body that indicated that he fired a gun. My son received at close range three gunshot wounds caused by two bullets. One bullet went through his left foot. The other bullet entered through the right flank, causing injury to several large blood vessels within the pelvis, and the other wound was on the anterior aspect of the right arm near the elbow. The officers involved in the so-called gun battle were not wounded, nor were they charged with any wrongdoing. The police department never showed me the gun that my son supposedly used in the so-called shoot-out, nor did they return any of his personal belongings. The police created a scenario that my son must have been on a suicide mission. I believe that the Birmingham Police Department was on a mission to eliminate young Black males from our society.

That situation took a piece of my heart and almost damaged my soul to the point of breaking my spirit. I operated in a state of denial for many years. What kept me going was that I told myself that Jermayne was searching to find his way back home. At the same time, my innermost spirit was telling me that he was in a place where he did not have to worry about being a Black male in a society that perceived him to be a threat. Jermayne gave his life to Christ at an early age, just like I had done. Yet his life was cut way too short like so many other young Black American males by the hands of White police. Jermayne was a quite sweet-spirited young man who wouldn't harm a flea. My heart will be forever broken. Every year when his birthday comes around since his death, my heart aches more than the year before, and I cannot hold back the river of tears. The empty feeling inside my soul makes me ask the questions: *Why, God? What went wrong? Will I ever know the real reason the police took my son's life?*

Jermayne loved football. When he was a young boy, he had aspirations of becoming a professional football player one day. He played basketball and football in middle school and high school. And he went on to play college football when he was a student at Lane College in Jackson, Tennessee, and later transferred to Miles College in Birmingham. Unlike me, Jermayne loved living in Birmingham. He had a strong attachment to my mother beyond grandmotherly love. My mom and dad nurtured him at a time in his life when his dad and I should have been there on a daily basis. I had to leave Jermayne with my parents after his dad and I got divorced. I was working toward my master's degree at that time and could not afford the extra child care expenses because Jermayne's dad was not being responsible at the time. My parents showered Jermayne with the same love that they gave my brother, my sister, and me. My dad tried to fill the void in Jermayne's life that he needed to receive from his dad. My divorced settlement gave his dad visitation rights which he did not uphold on a regular basis. So Jermayne looked up to my dad as his dad. When my dad died from a heart attack in March 1985, Jermayne was devastated. Jermayne was just thirteen years old. And thirteen years later, I was devastated by Jermayne's death. I am still trying to come to grips with the reality that he is no longer a beacon of light in the world. This reality caused me to reach a deeper level of my being and develop the kind of faith that no matter what I may face in the future, I had to believe that I could handle it.

When I reflected on the time frame of the murder of my son and the death of my father, the number thirteen must have had a significant meaning for me. From a Christian and a mathematical point of view, I believe that the number thirteen has a positive meaning—unlike the negative connotation attached to the number thirteen! If you analyze the numerical value of the initials JC (Jesus Christ) using the alphabetical order: *J* is the tenth letter of the alphabet, and *C* is the third letter of the alphabet. When you add up the value of these two letters, the sum is thirteen. Based on this analysis, there is nothing negative about the number thirteen. Researching the number thirteen further, I discovered that the number thirteen is connected to angel numbers. Exploring the basic vibrational energies of the digit one in the number thirteen of angel numbers represents a major change. The digit three in relation to the angel number thirteen refers to growth. The sum of the digits one and three is four. The number four is all about patience. The number one and the number thirteen both represent a new beginning. The murder of my son brought a major unexpected change to my life. But based on my signal from angel number thirteen, I would be able to weather the storm with patience and trust *and* experience a strong sense of my capacity for new growth and change.

However, there have been days in my life when I felt like a ship tackling the turbulence of the high seas. Having faith helped me navigate my way through the storms of life. My sister, Ann, died in September 1999—nine months after my son was killed. The cause of her death was pulmonary sarcoidosis, which caused serious damage to her lungs. She struggled to live a wholesome life with no complaints for twelve years after the onset of the disease. Sarcoidosis is a rare disease affecting mostly Black Americans. Based on research, sarcoidosis is a multisystem chronic inflammatory condition of unknown etiology. Treatment can help, but the condition cannot be cured.

Revealing my pain and suffering regarding the lessons of the past has helped me reclaim some hope to heal my wounds. I thank God for giving me a place to stand. I refuse to move backward. So as long as I am in the light, the movement must be forward regardless of the storms that may come my way. I decided not to let the murder of my son and the deaths of my father and sister define how I would look forward as I navigate the sea of life. I mentioned earlier that I know who I am and I accept me as I am. My heart may be broken, but I am going to keep moving forward anyhow. Just like a salmon swimming upstream. When I found myself in a place where I could not think about forgiveness for the wrong that was done to my son by the police, I realized that I could not stay stuck in the unforgiving mode. So I had to pray to find forgiveness in my heart to free myself of the pain and move beyond their mistake.

My Christian upbringing commands me to forgive the officer who made the mistake of murdering my son, but my human nature will never forget what was done. I know what the power of forgiveness brings. I also know that there are a lot of everyday people like me struggling with the injustice from the behavior of some White police not being held accountable for their unjust actions. In the absence of police protection, I am grateful to have the Holy Spirit within me as my shelter and refuge from any storm. I have found unlimited protection whenever I connect with the Spirit which shields me from all challenges. That same Spirit restored my strength and courage to face the injustices lingering in our society. I have discovered on this journey through life that you must be willing to die in order to live because death merely means change. My feelings of anger and revenge died within me when I found the courage to forgive the mistake of murder.

Just as Jesus prepared his followers for his death and resurrection during their last supper together when he told them that they would have troubles in the world, the Father would send them the Spirit of truth to live with them and be in them (John 14:16–17). As God's child experiencing the death of my son, I was made aware that I, too, have his Spirit living within to comfort me and flowing out of me to witness his peace. That Spirit protects me and bestows me with peace each and every day as I heal from that difficult challenge. However, even today, young Black American males lose their lives for no real just cause or reason from police brutality and hate groups. My wound is reopened each time the news media portrays the murder of a young Black American male for just being Black, which makes it even harder and more difficult for my heart to heal from my challenge.

In the midst of all the violence in America aimed at Black Americans and other people of color, I still hold onto hope for a better future. But the alarming rate of active hate groups and domestic terror organizations that continue to operate makes my dream for racial reconciliation seem remote. Shouldn't this matter be on the hearts and minds of all Americans to want to end hate? I imagine the idea of believing in the oneness of all life and actively standing up for the rights of all people to be treated with love, respect, and dignity was another remote dream of mine. The 2008 election of President Barack Obama should have been a major milestone for race relations in our nation, but his election sparked an unprecedented backlash from antigovernment extremists, and continued efforts were made by some politicians and naysayers to discredit his legitimacy as president. This was a clear sign to me that our nation was still raw and divided on racial issues. It caused me to wonder, What is it that makes it so hard to resolve issues about race relations? We all have the potential to become peacemakers, which is a matter of the heart. Charles Fillmore, founder of Unity Church in 1889, a church within the New Thought Movement, puts it this way: "A peacemaker is one who has the ability to say peace to the turbulent waves of thoughts and have them obey…who reduces to peace and harmony all the thoughts of strife, anger, and retaliation in their own mind." As a nation of people, we know the cause of racism and should take positive steps to promote healing and resolution. It is my belief that we all have a responsibility to contribute to world peace and live up to our potential by being the children that God created us to be. And acknowledging and honoring the Fourteenth Amendment of our Constitution would be a positive step toward moving forward. And if the powerful and the privileged develop a conscience to stop undermining the ideals of our Constitution that exploit prejudice to further their own ends, then the process of racial reconciliation, I believe, can be achieved.

My realization of the American dream of "human race equality" appeared to be in jeopardy because there were times when I felt that America did not love me. However, I will continue to have a deep love for America. America is the only home that I know. But the current state of our society continues to allow evil wills to linger in the environment that keeps us from becoming *E Pluribus Unum*." From what I have seen and witnessed, the political system is ugly and dirty. This makes me wonder why a perfectly good, almighty, and all-knowing God permits evil. According to what I read, theodicy, in its most common form, is the attempt to answer the question of why a good God permits the manifestation of evil. I know that God gave humans free will. I suppose that's why some humans misuse free will to spread moral evil through the political system and continue the portrayal of the United States of America as a White America. That evidence was very clear to me when Barack Obama was running for president in 2008 and he was being portrayed as not being a US-born citizen.

From that perspective, I could see that the political system does not equally represent all Americans, making it hard for me to understand why immoral and evil behavior goes unpunished or seems to go unpunished for far too long. But in spite of the ugly and evil wills, I do believe that we are all valuable individuals and were created for a good reason. Furthermore, I could not understand why political leaders were being voted into office who were not willing to stand up for American values and human rights for all the citizens of this great nation. I do have a favorable view, but neither am I a fan of how the political system and our government work. I have a much more favorable outlook and a stronger belief in exact science. Political analysts develop mathematical algorithms that make predictions to help sway the minds of Americans on major policy issues like equality and justice that do not favor all Americans. Most politicians tend to dance around the issues related to equality and justice. Because that would mean facing the demon called "racism." This means that the quality attributed to politics depends on the quality of the politicians who are elected to do what is right rather than just playing politics based on campaign contributions or loyalty to a political party.

Based on what I learned from my high school government class, the members of Congress are responsible for the operation of our constitutional system of government to the fullest extent. However, the left-right politics keeps the political system divided, leaving little to no path to the idea of centered politics. The idea that all people should be treated as equals and have the same political, economic, social, and civil rights is the ideal American dream. It is clear that the current political system needs amending to change what is wrong and corrupt. But it takes courage and conviction to go against the grain. Going against the grain would mean enforcing political and social equality for all Americans. According to the statement contained in the preamble of the Declaration of Independence, "All men are created equal." If I unpack that statement and focus on the word *men*, women are excluded. And focusing on when that statement was written, African Americans were not considered as humans. Today, however, I understand that equality should reflect the natural state of humanity, but at the same time, the concept of equality as it applies to all humanity becomes a complicated idea. Then maybe the statement in the preamble should be rewritten to state, "All humans are created equal." That's just part of my more optimistic view and dream about achieving racial reconciliation. I believe that the dream could be possible if we keep chipping away at the inequalities and our imperfections.

I have great hope for racial reconciliation. In spite of the evidence of the unforgettable day on September 15, 1963, at 10:22 a.m., that shamed the nation, I believe the evidence will eventually change our nation into "one nation, indivisible, with liberty and justice for all." I believe that true power is in our diversity and difference. Just like getting to the solution of any problem, racial reconciliation has to go through the process and stages necessary to be achieved and become a way of life. Every day that I make peace with myself and others is an opportunity for reconciliation. As I continue to practice forgiveness and compassion toward others, I will develop the capacity to forgive the mistakes of wrongdoings and to move toward restoration. According to the Yoruba proverbs, "You must have love in your heart before you can have hope."

Epilogue

Ten years ago, I began the writing process to tell my story. I never thought of myself as a writer or storyteller. My life as a retired educator was just kicking in when I attended a Writer's Boot Camp workshop for beginners. At that time, I did not want to believe that there were forces in our society trying to reverse the progress that our nation has made toward race relations, equality, and social justice. But it appeared that antigovernment extremists were attacking American values, freedom, and democracy at an alarming level. Active hate groups were on the rise. When I think back to the 2004 Democratic National Convention when Barack Obama spoke the words "There is not a Black America and White America and Latino America and Asian America—there's the United States of America," my vision of America was that which was no longer being shackled with Jim Crow laws and cultural conflict and had the hope of Dr. King's dreams for America being fulfilled. The progress and hard work that have brought some real change to our country are being threatened by some people who want to take the country back to a time when freedom and democracy were not shared by all Americans. The progress that has been made for lasting change toward a more perfect union appears to need more hard work and reconciled hearts.

It is hard for me to believe that after 240-plus years, the motto approved by Congress "E Pluribus Unum"—which means "Out of many, one," representing a vision of different people from different places and different cultures drawn together into "one nation, indivisible, with liberty and justice for all"—has yet to be accomplished. It appears that the political forces keep pulling us apart to make us "many out of one" instead of "one out of many." The motto leads me to believe that as a nation, we are in the company of people who have common goals for the common good of all. But the forces of bitterness, hatred, and evil wills conspire to hold back the way of peace, justice, and truth. When I look at the inscription "In God We Trust" on our US currency and coins, I wonder why that motto does not inspire us to look for ways to create and strengthen unity and equality for all.

My political viewpoint with respect to the current two-party political system needs to seek a balance between the views of the two parties for the common good of all. In many ways, the two-party system is beneficial for promoting the common good. At the same time, in a two-party system, coalition government is rarely formed because the two-party system is a dichotomous division of the political spectrum. My political spectrum is split between both liberal and conservative values. Similar to many Americans, I am left to choose one of the two parties to express my views and opinions. The majority party in Congress making the rules to perpetuate their power may not always be beneficial to my views and does not always rule to promote the common good of all. The 2017 ruling party took a sudden shift in political trends that threatened the government's stability, thereby not functioning as a government of, by, and for the people. The "winner takes all and loser gets nothing" rule does not work for the common good of all. I believe that the way to create a government of, by, and for the people is to relinquish old attitudes, habits, sins, and evil ways of thinking. I see that a more perfect union with continued progress toward lasting change means learning how to develop a pattern of living with changed attitudes that allows love to transform the hearts of Americans.

When I look back at the history of my ancestors, people of color are genetically coded for genius but have been programmed to self-destruct and taught that we must be authorized, qualified, and sanctioned by someone else. Thankfully today, I no longer believe that I must be validated by someone else to believe in myself; and I have learned to trust the built-in mechanism of information, protection, and guidance within. My mother instilled those values in my sister, my brother, and myself when we were young. But it took me a while to latch on to the idea, because there were times when I allowed the outside noise to get in the way. Since my mother's death in December 2014, at the age of ninety-two, I now understand what she meant when she told me that I was born with everything I needed to accomplish my mission and purpose in life. I gave my mother the nickname, "Big Annie," when I reached adulthood because she and my sister shared the same first name. But everybody called both of them "Ann." Big Annie was opinionated but always considerate of the feelings of others. My parents together built a family of love, strength, and togetherness. Their daily teachings provided a structure for Ann, Edmond, and me to strive to reach our fullest potential. Their examples about life will linger in my heart and soul forever. This helps me to believe in my dreams.

As a Black American, I do value, love, and cherish being Black. I cannot change the color of my skin. But as I continue to travel life's journey, I will try to radiate peace to all the people that I encounter. That is to say that I believe in all humanity. However, I do not like the negative way society and the media portray Black Americans. My ancestors helped to make America a great nation. I may not be a well-known or popular person to society and the world, but I am a regular person doing special things. Claiming my own humanity through God's grace has helped me with the process of healing from the racial wounds of the past and continue to deal with the unresolved racial issues today. I have a spiritual conviction that serves me in all situations, all day, every day, and in every way. I believe that the spirit is the light of truth, peace, joy, and love.-

About the Author

Dr. Ethel Madison Van Buren is a retired educator born in Birmingham, Alabama, and now residing in Metro Atlanta, Georgia. She has a bachelor's degree in mathematics and master's degree in guidance and counseling from Tennessee State University, Nashville, Tennessee, and a doctorate of education in instructional leadership from Argosy University. As an educator, she held several administrative positions at the higher education level at Tennessee State University and Miles College and served as a high school and junior college mathematics instructor.

Dr. Van Buren was listed on the Outstanding Young Women of America list in 1981. During her twenty-three years tenure with Dekalb County Schools, she received recognition for excellent service as a mentor to both students and new teachers and as a math teacher trainer, in addition to certificates of appreciation for her dedicated and valuable service to the students at Cross Keys High School and the Dekalb County School District.

Over the past fifty-plus years, Dr. Van Buren has echoed the message of this memoir to friends and colleagues. As a woman of faith, she lives her life trusting the Word of God. She is an active member of Cascade United Methodist Church of Atlanta, Georgia, where she serves on several worship ministries.

Dr. Van Buren is a divorcée and mother of one son (Jermayne Van Buren), now deceased, whom she misses and continues to hold his love dear to her heart.